COFFEE TIME TREATS

COFFEE TIME TREATS

*coffee cakes, sticky buns,
muffins and more*

RYLAND PETERS & SMALL

LONDON • NEW YORK

Designer Luana Gobbo
Picture Manager Christina Borsi
Copy Editor Miriam Catley
Head of Production Patricia Harrington
Art Director Leslie Harrington
Editorial Director Julia Charles
Indexer Hilary Bird

First published in 2014
by Ryland Peters & Small,
20–21 Jockey's Fields,
London WC1R 4BW
and
519 Broadway, 5th Floor,
New York NY 10012
www.rylandpeters.com

10 9 8 7 6 5 4 3 2 1

Text © Mickael Benichou, Susannah Blake,
Julian Day, Ross Dobson, Liz Franklin, Jane Mason,
Hannah Miles, Miisa Mink, Isidora Popovic,
Sarah Randell, Annie Rigg, Bea Vo, Laura
Washburn and Ryland, Peters & Small

Design and photographs © Ryland Peters
& Small 2014

ISBN: 978-1-84975-569-6

A CIP record for this book is available from the
British Library.

US Library of Congress cataloging-in publication
data has been applied for.

Printed and bound in China

Notes
- Both British (Metric) and American (Imperial
plus US cups) are included in these recipes for
your convenience, however it is important to
work with one set of measurements and not
alternate between the two within a recipe.
- All spoon measurements given are level unless
otherwise specified.
- All eggs are medium (UK) or large (US), unless
specified as large, in which case US extra-large
should be used. Uncooked or partially cooked eggs
should not be served to the very old, frail, young
children, pregnant women or those with
compromised immune systems.
- When a recipe calls for the grated zest of citrus
fruit, buy unwaxed fruit and wash well before
using. If you can only find treated fruit, scrub well
in warm soapy water before using.
- Ovens should be preheated to the specified
temperatures. We recommend using an oven
thermometer. If using a fan-assisted oven, adjust
temperatures according to the manufacturer's
instructions.

CONTENTS

INTRODUCTION

Coffee – made from ground roasted coffee beans – is loved and drunk the world over and there are a wealth of ways to make and serve it. This book provides recipes for delicious baked treats to enjoy alongside your daily cup of coffee, whether it's a morning pick-me-up or an after-dinner indulgence.

Ancient as tribes and irrepressibly modern, coffee adapts itself to time and place, encompassing the romantic, the industrious and the day-to-day. Its dynamic history is full of tales of passion and intrigue, yet it is also the drink of choice for breakfast, mid-morning office breaks and more often than not, the end to a formal dinner party. Prized for its enticing range of flavours and styles, used as a digestive, relied upon as a stimulant, coffee excites and focuses the brain along with the rest of the body. It brings us together over cups and conversation. Its aromatic allure can beckon us away from our daily business to a café or a quiet corner at home for a leisurely sip, a read of the newspaper and a view of the world.

However you like your coffee, and whatever your taste in sweet treats, you'll find the perfect bake here to accompany your morning espresso, mid-morning latte or after-dinner cappuccino. The recipes in this book are all intended to be eaten alongside a cup of coffee and are flavoured with ingredients that pair well with it, such as vanilla, chocolate, nuts, toffee, caramel, praline, nougat and warm spices like cinnamon and cardamom. And of course, coffee itself isn't just for enjoying as a drink; it's the perfect flavouring in its own right. Dark and bitter or subtly elusive, the taste of coffee is the perfect addition to many cookies, cakes, cheesecakes and brownies featured in this recipe collection.

Why not indulge in a little coffee culture at home? Make the perfect brew (see page 8) and choose from chewy cookies studded with chocolate, Italian-style biscotti speckled with nuts and dried fruit, sticky glazed pastries, moist muffins, indulgent brownies, light and creamy cheesecakes, sugar-dusted doughnuts, spiced buns and much more.

Whether you choose a short espresso, breakfast cappuccino, indulgent caffè latte, Americano or iced coffee, with more than 80 delicious recipes your favourite cup of coffee need never go unaccompanied again!

Many of the recipes within this book call for a basic pastry dough. While filo/phyllo and puff pastry are readily available, it is best to make your own choux and shortcrust pastry for cream puffs and tarts. These are the basic recipes that you will need.

Single quantity basic choux pastry/paste

65 g/½ cup plain/all-purpose flour
50 g/3 tablespoons unsalted butter, cut into cubes
75 ml/⅓ cup whole milk plus 75 ml/⅓ cup water or 150 ml/⅔ cup water
1 teaspoon caster/superfine sugar
a pinch of salt
2 eggs

Sift the flour onto a sheet of baking parchment twice to remove any lumps and to add as much air as possible. Heat the butter in a saucepan with the milk and water, sugar and salt until the butter has melted. As soon as the butter has melted remove the pan from the heat and quickly shoot the sifted flour in all in one go. It is important not to let the water heat for longer than it takes to melt the butter as this will evaporate some of the water and so there will be less liquid for the pastry.

Beat the mixture very hard with a wooden spoon or whisk until the dough forms a ball and no longer sticks to the sides of the pan and the pan is clean. At first the mixture will seem very wet but don't worry as it will come together after a few minutes once the flour absorbs the water. It is important to really beat the mixture well at this stage. Leave to cool for 5 minutes. Whisk the eggs in a separate bowl and then beat a small amount at a time into the pastry using a wooden spoon or a balloon whisk. The mixture will form a sticky paste which holds its shape when you lift the whisk up. When you first add the eggs and begin beating, the mixture will split slightly. This is normal and the pastry will come back together as you continue to beat. The mixture must be beaten hard at each stage. If the mixture is runny and does not hold its shape, unfortunately it cannot be used as it will not rise.

Single quantity basic shortcrust pastry

175 g/1½ sticks butter, softened
75 g/⅓ cup caster/granulated sugar
250 g/2 cups plain/all-purpose flour
1 egg yolk

Put the butter, sugar and flour in a large bowl and rub between your fingertips until the texture resembles fine breadcrumbs. (You can add orange or lemon zest at this point if desired.) Add the egg and work the mixture with your hands to a smooth paste. Wrap the dough in clingfilm/plastic wrap and refrigerate for about 30 minutes until firm.

Preheat the oven to 190°C (375°F) Gas 5.

Remove the dough from the refrigerator and roll out on a lightly floured surface. Line a tart pan with the pastry, gently press along the sides and into the corners and trim off any excess with a sharp knife. Prick the base in a few places with a fork and line the tart case with baking parchment. Fill the tart case with baking beans and bake blind in the preheated oven for 15–20 minutes.

Remove from the oven and set aside to cool before filling.

MAKING THE PERFECT COFFEE

In order to make great coffee at home, it helps to understand a few basic principles about the coffee itself and the coffee-making equipment. It's no good investing in elaborate or expensive kit if you're using unsuitable beans or the wrong grind. Here are some useful pointers to get you started.

Invest in freshly roasted beans from your local artisan supplier and always buy beans whole. Coffee beans have wonderful aromatic oils that are released when crushed, but the oils are also very fragile. Crushed too soon, the oils will dissipate and even worse, can go rancid. The expiration date on proper coffee beans is typically about a month and they should be ground only a few minutes before use. Store coffee beans in their foil pouch in the fridge or freezer, keeping the pouch airtight.

Invest in a good burr grinder; those same aromatic oils in coffee can be spoiled by high-speed, uneven grinders.

The simplest and most economical method for making coffee at home is the French press. For a 500-ml/2-cup capacity press you will need 500 ml/1 cup filtered water and 30 g/ 1 oz. high-quality filter coffee beans. Start to boil the water. Grind the coffee beans. You want a fairly coarse grind for filter coffee to allow for the extraction of the aromatics but not too much of the bitter oils. Pour into the

French press. Add the boiling water. Stir with a spoon for 30 seconds to let the coffee grounds swell up and release their oils. Add the lid and let sit for 3 minutes before gently plunging.

Alternatively, the stylish moka pot is common in many Italian homes and makes reasonable coffee at an affordable price. It comes in varying sizes from tiny single-serving pots to those that can brew 12 cups. The base of the pot holds a chamber into which water is poured. The pot is heated on the stove and as it warms, the steam pressure forces the hot water through the tube and into the chamber. From here it trickles into a top chamber, from which it is poured.

Finally, for those who love good espresso, an espresso pod machine is an option. These take small pods of vacuum-packed ground coffee and deliver the ideal dose of coffee, perfectly tamped. Depending on the model and the price you pay, they can make great coffee but the cost per cup can be fairly expensive, and the packaging does create extra waste.

Chapter 1

COOKIES & BISCOTTI

ULTIMATE CHOCOLATE CHIP COOKIES

The trick to the Ultimate Chocolate Chip Cookie is the obscene amount of butter and salt in the recipe – and of course, high-quality chocolate.

175 g/1¾ sticks unsalted butter,
   softened

½ teaspoon salt

40 g/2 tablespoons
   caster/superfine sugar

240 g/1 cup plus 2 tablespoons
   light brown soft sugar

1 egg

1 egg yolk

1½ teaspoons vanilla extract

240 g/1¾ cups plain/
   all-purpose flour

¼ teaspoon bicarbonate
   of/baking soda

25 ml/1 tablespoon milk

250 g/9 oz. high-quality
   dark/bittersweet chocolate,
   chopped into pea-sized pieces

*1–2 baking sheets, greased and
   lined with baking parchment*

Makes about 20

Using an electric mixer with paddle or beater attachment (or an electric whisk), beat the butter, salt and both sugars until the mixture is lightened in colour, fluffy in texture and increases in volume.

Beat the egg and egg yolk together in a small bowl. Slowly mix into the butter mixture and beat until thoroughly combined. Add the vanilla extract and mix.

Sift together the flour and bicarbonate of/baking soda. Add half the flour mixture to the butter mixture and beat until just combined. Add the milk and beat until just combined. Add the remaining flour mixture and beat until just combined.

Add the chopped chocolate to the dough and mix until thoroughly combined.

Using 2 spoons, place large dollops of dough (about 40 g/ 1½ oz.) onto the prepared baking sheets, spaced well apart. (There's no need to flatten them and they will spread on baking.) Refrigerate for 20–25 minutes until thoroughly chilled. (At this point, you can also pop them in the freezer, freeze them for 2 hours, then place the dough balls in an airtight freezer bag and freeze for up to 2 weeks, for baking at a later date. Defrost for 15 minutes before baking.)

Preheat the oven to 180°C (350°F) Gas 4.

When the dough is thoroughly chilled, put the baking sheets in the preheated oven and bake for 9–13 minutes. The cookies are done when the tops don't look shiny or wet any more. Remove from the oven and let cool on the baking sheets for 5 minutes. Transfer the cookies to a wire rack and let rest until ready to eat or eat them hot, straight out of the oven.

PRUNE, CINNAMON AND TOASTED WALNUT COOKIES WITH CINNAMON ICING

Agen prunes are a juicy and delicious addition to these chewy cookies, but raisins would also be a good choice. If you are making the cookies at Christmastime or are feeling decadent, substitute half the water in the icing with Armagnac.

75 g/½ cup walnut pieces

100 g/6½ tablespoons unsalted butter, softened

150 g/¾ cup packed light brown soft sugar

1 large egg, lightly beaten

2 tablespoons cream cheese

75 g/⅔ cup light brown/whole-wheat and 75 g/⅔ cup white self-raising/rising flour (or use all white flour)

2 teaspoons ground cinnamon

a pinch of salt

125 g/1 cup pitted, soft Agen prunes, snipped into small pieces

50 g/¼ cup icing/confectioners' sugar

2 or 3 pinches of ground cinnamon

2 baking sheets, greased

Makes about 20

Preheat the oven to 200°C (400°F) Gas 6.

Spread the walnuts on a baking sheet and toast in the preheated oven for 5 minutes, then let cool.

Put the butter and sugar in an electric mixer (or use a large mixing bowl and an electric whisk) and beat until light and fluffy. Add the egg and cream cheese and mix again to combine. Sift in the flours (add any bran left in the sieve/strainer from the brown/whole-wheat flour, if using), the cinnamon and salt and mix again. Fold in the toasted walnuts and prunes with a large metal spoon.

Drop craggy mounds of the mixture onto the prepared baking sheets – about 1 rounded dessertspoonful each. Leave room between them to allow the cookies to spread as they bake; 6 or 7 per baking sheet is about right, so you will need to cook them in batches. Bake the cookies in the preheated oven for 10–12 minutes, or until golden. Let cool for a few minutes, then transfer to a wire rack to cool completely.

To make the cinnamon icing, sift the icing/confectioners' sugar and cinnamon into a small bowl. Add 2 teaspoons cold water and mix – you want a drizzling consistency, so add a few more drops of water if needed. Drizzle a little icing over each cookie and let set.

COFFEE, MACADAMIA AND WHITE CHOCOLATE CHUNK COOKIES

These big, fat, chunky, chewy cookies are subtly flavoured with coffee and studded with chunks of white chocolate and macadamia nuts.

115 g/1 stick unsalted butter, at room temperature

200 g/1 scant cup caster/granulated sugar

1 egg

1 tablespoon instant coffee granules dissolved in 1½ tablespoons just-boiled water

100 g/¾ cup macadamia nuts

100 g/¾ cup white chocolate, roughly chopped

100 g/⅔ cup self-raising/rising flour

100 g/⅔ cup plain/all-purpose flour

2 baking sheets, greased

Makes about 15

Preheat the oven to 190°C (375°F) Gas 5.

Beat together the butter and sugar until creamy, then beat in the egg, followed by the coffee. Stir in the macadamia nuts and chocolate and mix together.

Combine the flours and sift over the cookie mixture, then stir until thoroughly combined.

Drop heaped tablespoonfuls of the mixture on to the baking sheets, spacing them well apart. Bake for about 10 minutes until pale golden and slightly puffed up.

Leave the cookies to firm up for a few minutes, then transfer to a wire rack to cool.

PECAN AND CRANBERRY COOKIES

Lovely sweet pecan nuts contrasting with the sharpness of dried cranberries. This is a perfect winter cookie.

110 g/1 stick unsalted butter, at room temperature

145 g/¾ cup light brown soft sugar

1 tablespoon golden syrup

a few drops of vanilla extract

1 egg

200 g/1½ cups plain/all-purpose flour

½ teaspoon baking powder

30 g/¼ cup shelled pecan nuts, chopped

30 g/¼ cup dried cranberries

1–2 baking sheets, greased and lined with baking parchment

Makes about 12

Cream the butter and sugar in a mixing bowl until light and fluffy. Add the syrup, vanilla and egg and mix well. Mix the flour and baking powder together in a separate bowl, then mix into the wet ingredients. Finally, mix in the pecans and cranberries.

Roll the dough into a log 5 cm/2 inches in diameter, wrap in clingfilm/plastic wrap and refrigerate for about 1 hour.

Preheat the oven to 170°C (325°F) Gas 3. Remove the dough from the fridge and unwrap it. Cut into discs about 2 cm/¾ inch thick. Arrange the discs on the prepared baking sheet(s), spacing them well apart as they will spread when they are baking.

Bake in the preheated oven for about 20–25 minutes until the cookies are pale gold. Remove from the oven and leave to cool for a few minutes, then serve warm. Store in an airtight container for up to 1 week.

ORANGE CRUSH COOKIES

This may look like a classic chocolate chip cookie but take a bite and your taste buds will get a real treat. With orange extract and orange zest, this recipe is irresistible. Orange and dark/bittersweet chocolate are a match made in heaven and work magically in a cookie.

120 g/1 stick unsalted butter, at room temperature and chopped
100 g/½ cup caster/granulated sugar
40 g/3½ tablespoons muscovado or soft brown sugar
2 teaspoons pure vanilla extract
1 drop of orange extract or orange flower water
2 teaspoons single/light cream
1 egg
180 g/1⅓ cups plain/all-purpose flour
1 teaspoon cocoa powder
½ teaspoon baking powder
¼ teaspoon salt
85 g/½ cup dark/bittersweet chocolate chips
finely grated zest of ½ orange

1–2 baking sheets, greased and lined with baking parchment

Makes about 25

Put the butter in a bowl and beat with a wooden spoon until very soft. Beat in the sugars until well incorporated and creamy, then add the vanilla extract, orange extract or flower water, cream and egg and beat in. Gradually sift in the flour, cocoa powder, baking powder and salt and mix until combined. Finally, mix in the chocolate chips and orange zest.

Cover and refrigerate for 30 minutes.

Preheat the oven to 170°C (325°F) Gas 3.

Remove the bowl from the fridge. Lightly flour a clean work surface and roll the chilled dough out into a sausage roughly 30 cm/12 inches long. Cut the dough into about 25 equal slices and arrange on the prepared baking sheets.

Bake in the preheated oven for about 15–20 minutes until browned. Allow the cookies to cool on the baking sheets for 5 minutes, then transfer to a wire rack to finish cooling.

WHITE CHOCOLATE AND FIG COOKIES

These are super indulgent cookies – soft, chewy and fruity, with creamy white chocolate chips. Heavenly. Try to buy soft, dried figs as they are the easiest to bake with. If, however, you can only find dried figs, you will have to cut off their hard stalks before you add them to the cookie dough.

50 g/3 tablespoons unsalted butter, at room temperature

80 g/⅓ cup plus 1 tablespoon golden caster/granulated sugar

a few drops of vanilla extract

1 egg

70 g/½ cup soft, dried figs, chopped

50 g/⅓ cup white chocolate, chopped (or use chips)

130 g/1 cup plain/all-purpose flour

1½ teaspoons baking powder

1–2 baking sheets, greased and lined with baking parchment

Makes about 15

Preheat the oven to 160°C (325°F) Gas 3.

Cream the butter and sugar in a mixing bowl until light and fluffy. Add the vanilla and egg and mix well. Stir in the figs and chopped chocolate. Mix the flour and baking powder together in a separate bowl, then gently fold into the wet ingredients.

Take a generous teaspoon of the cookie dough and place on one of the prepared baking sheets. Flatten slightly, then repeat with the remaining dough, spacing the dough balls well apart as they will spread when they are baking.

Bake in the preheated oven for about 25 minutes, or until the cookies are pale gold. Remove from the oven and leave to cool for a few minutes. Store in an airtight container for up to 1 week.

GINGER AND CHILLI CARAMEL COOKIES

Explore your artistic side when it comes to decorating these cookies drizzled with hot caramel. With a generous dose of crystallized ginger and bit of chilli heat, they are not for the faint-hearted and are super-addictive!

50 g/3 tablespoons unsalted
    butter, at room temperature
100 g/½ cup golden
    caster/granulated sugar
1 egg
50 g/½ cup crystallized ginger,
    finely chopped
130 g/1 cup plain/all-purpose
    flour
1½ teaspoons baking powder
2 teaspoons ground ginger

Chilli caramel
100 g/½ cup golden
    caster/granulated sugar
a pinch of ground cayenne
    pepper or hot chilli powder
    (or more if you like the heat!)

1–2 baking sheets, greased

Makes about 15

Preheat the oven to 160°C (325°F) Gas 3.

Cream the butter and sugar in a mixing bowl until light and fluffy. Add the egg and mix well, then stir in the crystallized ginger. Mix the flour, baking powder and ground ginger in a separate bowl, then gently fold into the wet ingredients.

Take a generous teaspoon of the dough and place on one of the prepared baking sheets. Flatten it slightly, then repeat this process with the remaining dough, spacing the dough balls well apart as they will spread when they are baking.

Bake in the preheated oven for about 25 minutes, or until the cookies are golden. Remove from the oven and leave to cool while you make the chilli caramel.

To make the chilli caramel, put the sugar in a heavy-based saucepan over medium heat. The sugar can burn quite easily (which can render the caramel bitter), so stir it often and keep a close eye on it. After a few minutes, the sugar should have completely melted. Remove from the heat and stir in the pepper or chilli powder. Be very careful when handling caramel as it can easily burn you. Use it immediately before it starts to harden.

Using a spoon, drizzle the caramel over the cookies any way you like. The caramel sets extremely quickly. When it has set, remove the cookies from the baking sheet. Store in an airtight container for up to 1 week, but be warned that the caramel can seep into the cookies in particularly humid conditions.

CARAMEL ALMOND COOKIES

With a crisp, buttery cookie base and a coating of flaky almonds in caramel, these cookies are delicious – and they make the perfect accompaniment to a mid-morning espresso.

Cookie base

90 g/6 tablespoons butter, softened

60 g/⅓ cup icing/confectioners' sugar

1 egg yolk

150 g/1 cup plus 2 tablespoons plain/all-purpose flour

Almond topping

60 g/4 tablespoons butter

100 g/½ cup caster/granulated sugar

2 tablespoons honey

3–4 tablespoons flaked toasted almonds

a shallow baking sheet, approx 20 x 30 cm/ 8 x 12 inches

Makes about 20

Preheat the oven to 180°C (350°F) Gas 4.

First make the cookie base. Cream the butter and icing/confectioners' sugar together until smooth. Stir in the egg yolk. Work in the flour to form a soft dough and roll out on a lightly floured work surface to fit the baking sheet. Lift it carefully into the baking sheet.

To make the almond topping, put the butter in a small saucepan with the sugar and honey and heat gently until the butter has melted and the sugar has dissolved. Bubble for 3–4 minutes until the mixture is golden. Stir in the flaked almonds. Spread the mixture evenly over the cookie base and bake for about 8 minutes, until the cookie base and topping are both golden. Leave to cool a little in the baking sheet, and then cut into rectangles and transfer to a wire rack until completely cold. Store in an airtight tin.

HAZELNUT MACAROONS

These cookies are dairy- and gluten-free. If you prefer, you can use ground almonds in place of the rice flour – it will make the macaroons just a touch softer. They are crunchy on the outside, chewy in the middle, and very, very nutty.

160 g/1 cup plus 2 tablespoons
   blanched hazelnuts
2 egg whites
160 g/¾ cup golden
   caster/granulated sugar
40 g/⅓ cup rice flour (or ground
   almonds)
a few drops of vanilla extract

*a baking sheet, greased and
   lined with baking parchment*

Makes about 20

Preheat the oven to 130°C (250°F) Gas ½.

Put the hazelnuts on a baking sheet and roast in the preheated oven for about 15 minutes, or until very pale gold. Remove from the oven and turn off the heat. Grind them finely in a spice grinder or food processor, leaving a few chunkier pieces.

In a mixing bowl, mix the egg whites and sugar to combine, then add the ground hazelnuts, rice flour and vanilla. Cover with clingfilm/plastic wrap and refrigerate for 30 minutes.

Preheat the oven to 130°C (250°F) Gas ½.

Take the mixture out of the fridge and stir through with a spoon. Take a generous teaspoon of the dough and place on the prepared baking sheet. Flatten it slightly, then repeat this process with the remaining dough, spacing the dough balls slightly apart as they may spread when they are baking.

Bake in the preheated oven for about 25 minutes, or until the macaroons are very pale gold. They should still be slightly soft in the middle. Remove from the oven and leave to cool for a few minutes. Store in an airtight container for up to 1 week.

LADIES' KISSES

Ladies' kisses cookies have a delicious texture and an exquisite lingering flavour – just like the loveliest kind of kiss should have! To save time, you could cheat and use Nutella for the filling.

100 g/6½ tablespoons unsalted butter, softened

100 g/½ cup caster/granulated sugar

100 g/⅔ cup ground almonds

100 g/¾ plus 1 tablespoon flour

Chocolate butter filling

50 g/2 oz. dark/bittersweet chocolate, broken into pieces

20 g/4 teaspoons unsalted butter

1–2 baking sheets, greased and lined with baking parchment

Makes 10

Preheat the oven to 180°C (350°F) Gas 4.

Beat the butter and sugar together until smooth. Work in the ground almonds and flour until the mixture forms a stiff dough. Break off 20 pieces the size of walnuts and form into balls. Arrange on baking sheets, leaving a little room between each. Bake in

the preheated oven for 10 minutes, until golden. Remove from the oven and transfer to a wire rack to cool.

Meanwhile, melt the chocolate in a bowl set over a saucepan of gently simmering water (or microwave on full power for 1–2 minutes, stirring halfway through). Remove from the heat, stir in the butter and leave to cool. When the cookies are cool, use the chocolate butter to sandwich them together.

TOASTED HAZELNUT FLORENTINES

Florentines are lovely with morning coffee, but make delicious petit fours to serve after dinner too – and they taste every bit as lovely as they look. Take care to be very precise with the measurements.

60 g/4 tablespoons unsalted butter

60 g/5 tablespoons caster/granulated sugar

1 tablespoon runny honey

60 g/½ cup plain/all-purpose flour

50 g/⅓ cup chopped mixed/candied citrus peel

50 g/⅓ cup glacé cherries, finely chopped

50 g/⅓ cup toasted hazelnuts, finely chopped

1 teaspoon freshly squeezed lemon juice

1 tablespoon double/heavy cream

200 g/7 oz. dark/bittersweet chocolate, broken into pieces

a baking sheet, greased and lined with baking parchment

Makes about 15

Preheat the oven to 180°C (350°F) Gas 4.

Melt the butter, sugar and honey together in a small saucepan over a gentle heat. Cool slightly and stir in the remaining ingredients except the chocolate.

Drop teaspoonfuls of the mixture onto the baking sheet, allowing a little room between each for spreading. Bake for 8–10 minutes, until golden. Leave to cool slightly and then transfer to a wire rack.

When the cookies are cold, melt the chocolate in a bowl set over a saucepan of gently simmering water (or microwave on full power for 1–2 minutes, stirring halfway through). Spread one side of each Florentine with a layer of chocolate and leave on the wire rack until set.

AMARETTI BISCUITS

These versatile little almond-flavoured cookies are crunchy on the outside and chewy on the inside. Perfect to serve with coffee anytime, they also make a great teatime treat when sandwiched together with buttercream, or serve them with the best coffee or vanilla ice cream as a dessert.

2 egg whites
175 g/¾ cup plus 2 tablespoons
    caster/granulated sugar
200 g/1⅓ cups ground almonds
1 tablespoon Amaretto liqueur
30 whole shelled almonds, to
    decorate

*a piping bag fitted with a
    12-mm/½-inch nozzle/tip
    (optional)*

*2 baking sheets, greased and
    lined with baking parchment*

Makes about 30

Preheat the oven to 170°C (325°F) Gas 3.

In a clean, grease-free bowl, whisk the egg whites using an electric hand whisk until firm peaks are formed. Add the sugar, ground almonds and Amaretto and gently fold into the egg whites until you have a smooth paste.

Fill the piping bag (if using) with the mixture and squeeze approximate 4-cm/1½-inch circles onto the prepared baking sheets. This can also be done using 2 dessertspoons – one to scoop the mixture from the bowl and the other to scrape it off onto the baking sheet. Place a whole almond in the centre of each cookie and bake in the preheated oven for 20 minutes or until risen, pale golden and they have small cracks over the surface. Remove the cookies from the oven and allow them to cool on the baking sheet.

The cookies will keep for 7–10 days in an airtight container.

CHOCOLATE PEANUT BUTTER BISCOTTI

Try dunking these divine biscotti in your favourite brew – the irresistible combination of chocolate and peanut butter pairs beautifully with coffee.

300 g/2 cups plain/all-purpose flour

1½ teaspoons baking powder

1½ teaspoons salt

100 g/½ cup light brown soft/granulated sugar

40 g/2 tablespoons natural cocoa powder (not Dutch-process)

40 g/2 tablespoons golden syrup

3 tablespoons sunflower oil

2 eggs

2 teaspoons water

1 teaspoon vanilla extract

80 g/⅔ cup shelled whole peanuts (unsalted or honey roasted)

80 g/3 oz. high-quality dark/bittersweet chocolate, chopped into pea-sized pieces

caster/superfine sugar, for sprinkling

70 g/½ cup peanut butter (crunchy or smooth)

a baking sheet, greased and lined with baking parchment

Makes about 30

Put the flour, baking powder, salt, sugar and cocoa powder in a large mixing bowl and mix until well combined.

Put the syrup, oil, eggs, water and vanilla extract in a separate bowl and whisk until well combined. Add to the dry mixture and mix until just combined and no trace of dry flour remains. Add the peanuts and chocolate and incorporate until combined.

Bring the dough together into a ball, wrap in clingfilm/plastic wrap and refrigerate for 1 hour.

Preheat the oven to 145°C (290°F) Gas 1½.

Sprinkle the work surface liberally with caster/granulated sugar. Transfer the dough to the work surface and flatten roughly with your hands. Dot spoonfuls of peanut butter all over the dough. Lightly roll the dough into a log about 6 cm/2½ inches wide and 2 cm/1 inch high (it will spread when baking). Try to encase the peanut butter inside the log, as it can burn if exposed directly to the heat of the oven.

Place the log on the prepared baking sheet and bake in the preheated oven for 25–40 minutes until the top is completely hardened, and when tapped, feels sturdy and not squishy inside. Remove from the oven and let cool for 30 minutes. Turn the oven temperature down to 135°C (265°F) Gas 1.

Slice the cooled log, diagonally, into 1-cm/½-inch wide batons. Lay all the batons flat on the same baking sheet and bake for 10–15 minutes until nice and dry, then flip all the biscotti over and bake again for 10–15 minutes. Remove from the oven and let cool on the baking sheet for 1 minute.

Transfer the biscotti to a wire rack and let cool completely. Store in an airtight container for up to 1 month.

COFFEE BEAN AND CHERRY BISCOTTI

These long, elegant, crisp Italian cookies studded with chocolate-covered coffee beans and dried cherries are the perfect treat for coffee lovers to enjoy with their mid-morning brew.

85 g/½ cup plain/all-purpose
   flour
85 g/½ cup self-raising/rising
   flour
60 g/⅓ cup polenta
85 g/½ cup caster/granulated
   sugar
2 eggs
1 teaspoon vanilla extract
50 g/⅓ cup dried cherries
50 g/⅓ cup chocolate-covered
   coffee beans
30 g/¼ cup blanched almonds

a baking sheet, greased

Makes about 20

Preheat the oven to 160°C (325°F) Gas 3.

Sift together the plain/all-purpose and self-raising/rising flours, polenta and sugar into a large bowl and make a well in the centre.

Beat together the eggs and vanilla extract and pour into the dry ingredients. Add the cherries, coffee beans and almonds and stir. Knead gently until the mixture comes together into a sticky dough.

Shape the dough into a log about 20 x 10 x 2 cm/ 8 x 4 x 1 inches and put on the prepared baking sheet. Bake for about 30 minutes until golden.

Remove from the oven (leaving the oven on) and leave to cool for about 5 minutes, then transfer to a chopping board and cut into slices 7 mm–1 cm/½-inch thick. Arrange the slices on the baking sheet and bake for a further 15–20 minutes, turning halfway through, until crisp and golden.

Remove from the oven, transfer to a wire rack and let cool.

HAZELNUT, ORANGE AND MARSALA RAISIN BISCOTTI

Biscotti keep for a month or so, making them a great standby. Dip them in a good espresso, as you eat them.

100 g/⅔ cup raisins

2 tablespoons Marsala

250 g/2 cups self-raising/rising flour

3 tablespoons cocoa powder

1 teaspoon baking powder

150 g/¾ cup caster/granulated sugar

2 large eggs, lightly beaten

finely grated zest of 1 large orange

100 g/⅔ cup blanched hazelnuts, roughly chopped

2 baking sheets, greased and lined with baking parchment

Makes about 30

Preheat the oven to 180°C (350°F) Gas 4.

Put the raisins in a small bowl with the Marsala, stir and let soak for at least 15 minutes.

Tip the flour, cocoa, baking powder and sugar into a food processor and whiz to mix. Add the beaten eggs and orange zest and whiz again for a couple of minutes until the mixture resembles coarse breadcrumbs. Tip the mixture into a mixing bowl and add the raisins and their liquid, and the chopped hazelnuts.

Using a spatula or wooden spoon, mix and knead everything together in the bowl until it starts to clump together – this will take a few minutes. Tip the dough out onto a lightly floured work surface and bring together into a ball with your hands.

Halve the dough and briefly knead each half. Roll each one into a 20-cm/8-inch long log. Put both logs onto one of the prepared baking sheets, leaving about 8–10 cm/4 inches between them to allow them to spread as they bake. Bake in the preheated oven for 35 minutes.

Remove the baked logs from the oven and let cool for 15 minutes, or until they are cool enough to handle. Meanwhile, reduce the oven temperature to 150°C (300°F) Gas 2.

Using a serrated bread knife, slice the logs on the diagonal into 1-cm/⅜-inch-thick slices. You should get about 15 slices from each log. Discard the ends.

Arrange the slices on the 2 baking sheets in a single layer and bake them for a further 20 minutes to dry them out. Let cool on wire racks.

RASPBERRY TWISTS

These cookies are very pleasing to look at, served on a tray for an elegant afternoon coffee. Raspberry jam/jelly works well because of the colour contrast with the cookie dough, but you can also use marmalade here.

200 g/1 stick plus 6 tablespoons unsalted butter, softened at room temperature
125 g/⅔ cup caster/granulated sugar
1 egg
1 teaspoon vanilla extract
250 g/2 cups plain/all-purpose flour
1 teaspoon baking powder
150 g/⅔ cup raspberry jam/jelly or marmalade
icing/confectioners' sugar, for dusting

2–3 baking sheets, greased and lined with baking parchment

Makes 35–40

Put the butter and sugar in a mixing bowl and cream it with a wooden spoon or handheld whisk until pale and fluffy. Add the egg and mix well. Add the vanilla extract, flour and baking powder and mix well to form a dough.

Roll into a ball, then wrap in clingfilm/plastic wrap and refrigerate for at least 1 hour.

Preheat the oven to 180°C (350°F) Gas 4.

Take the dough out of the refrigerator and remove the clingfilm/plastic wrap. Roll the dough out on a well floured surface, with a rolling pin, until about 35 x 40 cm/14 x 16 inches.

Spread the jam/jelly evenly over the dough, leaving a 2-cm/1-inch border around the edge. Roll the dough up from a long side. Cut into roughly 1-cm/½-inch rolls. Arrange the rolls, cut-side down, on the prepared baking sheets, leaving plenty of space between them, as they will spread when they bake.

Bake in the preheated oven for 12–15 minutes, until golden.

Let cool a little before transferring to a wire rack to cool completely. Dust with icing/confectioners' sugar just before serving.

Chapter 2

BROWNIES, BARS & SLICES

SALTED CARAMEL SWIRL BROWNIES

With swirls of luscious caramel running through them, these brownies are definitely in the grown-up league. Serve warm.

100 g/1 cup shelled pecans

225 g/8 oz. dark/bittersweet chocolate, chopped

150 g/1 stick plus 2 tablespoons unsalted butter, diced

225 g/1 cup caster/granulated sugar

4 eggs, lightly beaten

1 teaspoon vanilla extract

125 g/1 cup plain/all-purpose flour

a pinch of salt

Salted caramel

50 g/¼ cup caster/granulated sugar

50 g/¼ cup light muscovado/light brown sugar

2 tablespoons unsalted butter

75 ml/⅓ cup double/heavy cream

½ teaspoon sea salt flakes

a 23-cm/9-inch square baking pan, greased and lined with baking parchment

Makes 25

Make the salted caramel first. Put the caster/granulated sugar and 2 tablespoons water in a small saucepan over low heat and let the sugar dissolve completely. Bring to the boil, then cook until the syrup turns to an amber-coloured caramel. Remove from the heat and add the muscovado/brown sugar, butter and cream. Stir to dissolve, then return to the low heat and simmer for 3–4 minutes until the caramel has thickened and will coat the back of a spoon. Remove from the heat, add the salt, pour into a bowl and leave until completely cold and thick.

Preheat the oven to 170°C (325°F) Gas 3.

Tip the pecans onto a baking sheet and lightly toast in the preheated oven for 5 minutes. Roughly chop and leave to cool. Leave the oven on for the brownies.

Put the chocolate and butter in a heatproof bowl set over a saucepan of barely simmering water. Stir until smooth and thoroughly combined. Leave to cool slightly.

In a separate bowl, whisk the sugar, eggs and vanilla extract. Add the melted chocolate mixture and stir until combined. Sift the flour and salt into the bowl and fold in until well incorporated, then stir in the pecans.

Pour half the mixture into the prepared baking pan and spread level. Drizzle half the salted caramel over the top, then pour the remaining mixture over that. Finish by drizzling the remaining salted caramel on top, then use a round-bladed knife to swirl the mixtures together. Tap the pan on the work surface to level the mixture and bake on the middle shelf of the preheated oven for 20–25 minutes.

Remove from the oven and let cool completely in the pan before removing from the pan and cutting into 25 squares.

PECAN CHEESECAKE SWIRL BROWNIES

These Pecan Cheesecake Swirl Brownies are gorgeous to look at and won't disappoint any brownie lover. Don't overcook them, as you want them to have slightly soft, moist centres.

100 g/⅔ cup pecan halves

100 g/3½ oz. dark/bittersweet chocolate (70% cocoa solids), broken into pieces

100 g/6½ tablespoons unsalted butter, softened

200 g/1 cup light muscovado or packed light brown soft sugar

2 eggs, lightly beaten

100 g/¾ cup plain/all-purpose flour, sifted

Cheesecake swirl

1 egg

150 g/5 oz. cream cheese

3 tablespoons caster/granulated sugar

1 tablespoon plain/all-purpose flour

an 18-cm/7-inch square pan, greased and lined with baking parchment

Makes 16

Preheat the oven to 180°C (350°F) Gas 4.

Spread the pecans on a baking sheet and toast in the preheated oven for 10 minutes, then let cool.

Melt the chocolate pieces in a small heatproof bowl set over a pan of barely simmering water. Remove the bowl from the heat and let cool a little.

Roughly chop the toasted pecans.

Put the butter and sugar in an electric mixer (or use a large mixing bowl and an electric whisk) and beat until combined. Gradually add the beaten eggs, still mixing. Tip in the flour and add the slightly cooled melted chocolate. Mix again until combined. Using a large metal spoon, fold in the chopped pecans.

To make the cheesecake swirl, whisk all the ingredients together in a bowl until combined.

Tip the chocolate mixture into the prepared pan and spread it evenly with a spatula. Drop blobs of the cheesecake mixture on top and, using a skewer or the end of a teaspoon, briefly swirl the cheesecake mixture into the top of the chocolate layer.

Bake the brownies in the preheated oven for 25 minutes. Let cool completely before cutting into 16 squares.

COFFEE LOVER'S BROWNIES

Chocolate and coffee make for a heavenly after-dinner treat. In this simple recipe, the coffee enhances the taste of the chocolate and gives the brownie a sophisticated depth of flavour.

225 g/8 oz. dark/bittersweet chocolate (55% cocoa), chopped

200 g/1 stick plus 6 tablespoons tablespoons unsalted butter, chopped

4 eggs

130 g/⅔ cup caster/granulated sugar

125 g/1 scant cup plain/all-purpose flour

1½ tablespoons instant coffee or espresso granules

a 20-cm/8-inch square baking pan, greased and dusted with flour

Makes 6–8

Preheat the oven to 170°C (325°F) Gas 3.

Put the chocolate and butter in a heatproof bowl set over a saucepan of barely simmering water. Do not let the base of the bowl touch the water. Allow to melt, stirring occasionally, until completely smooth. Remove from the heat.

In a separate bowl, whisk the eggs and sugar for 1–2 minutes. Sift in the flour, add the coffee and whisk again to mix. Pour the chocolate mixture in and mix well with a wooden spoon.

Spoon the mixture into the prepared baking pan, spread level with a spatula and bake in the preheated oven for about 25 minutes. Allow the brownies to cool in the pan for a few minutes, then turn out onto a wire rack to cool completely.

Serve at room temperature, cut into equal portions.

CHOCOLATE FUDGE BROWNIES

A genuine brownie should first and foremost taste of chocolate. There should be undertones of coffee and vanilla and it should be dark and nutty, with a fudge-like centre and a firm, slightly crispy outer surface.

3 eggs

220 g/1 cup plus 2 tablespoons caster/granulated sugar

300 g/10 oz. dark/bittersweet chocolate, broken into pieces

220 g/2 sticks salted butter

2 tablespoons vanilla extract

1 tablespoon instant coffee granules

2 tablespoons water, boiling

70 g/½ cup self-raising/ rising flour

100 g/⅔ cup chopped walnuts

a 34 x 20 x 3-cm/14 x 8 x 1¼-inch baking pan, greased and lined with baking parchment

Makes 20

Preheat the oven to 180°C (350°F) Gas 4.

Put the eggs and sugar in a large bowl. With a balloon whisk or an electric hand whisk, whisk together until smooth, very thick and pale, and no sugar is left in the base of the bowl.

Melt the chocolate and butter in a heatproof bowl set over a pan of simmering water. Do not let the base of the bowl touch the water. Stir frequently until smooth and well mixed. Put the vanilla extract and coffee granules in a cup, add the boiling water and stir vigorously until dissolved and smooth. Add the melted chocolate and butter to the egg and sugar mix, followed by the coffee infusion and stir to mix. Fold in the flour, then add the walnuts and gently stir through.

Spoon the mixture into the prepared baking pan and bake in the preheated oven for 35–40 minutes until just firm to the touch. Remove the brownies from the oven and let cool in the pan, then turn out onto a wire rack. They are best eaten warm or at room temperature but are easier to slice when chilled. To portion, refrigerate the brownies until chilled, then slice with a sharp knife.

The brownies will keep in an airtight container at room temperature for 7–10 days. They are also good for home freezing.

WHITE CHOCOLATE AND COFFEE TRUFFLE BROWNIES

Here, the brownie is elevated to new heights of indulgence with the addition of white chocolate – tiny bursts of sweetness that contrast perfectly with the hints of bitter coffee. These decadent brownies are the ultimate accompaniment to your favourite black brew.

240 g/8 oz. dark/bittersweet chocolate (at least 70% cocoa solids)

100 g/6½ tablespoons unsalted butter

2 teaspoons instant coffee granules

3 tablespoons boiling water

3 eggs

135 g/⅔ cup golden caster/granulated sugar

55 g/½ cup plain/all-purpose flour

70 g/2½ oz. white chocolate, chopped (or use chips)

cocoa powder, to dust

an 18-cm/8-inch square baking pan, greased and lined with baking parchment

Makes 8–10 squares

Preheat the oven to 150°C (300°F) Gas 2.

Put the chocolate and butter in a heatproof bowl over a saucepan of barely simmering water. Do not let the base of the bowl touch the water. Stir until melted. Set aside to cool.

Put the instant coffee and boiling water in a cup and stir until dissolved. Set aside.

Put the eggs and sugar in a mixing bowl and whisk until pale and creamy. Stir in the coffee. Sift in the flour and fold in gently, then fold in the molten chocolate and mix until smooth. Finally, stir in the chopped chocolate.

Pour the batter into the prepared baking pan and bake in the preheated oven for about 15 minutes. The brownies should have risen slightly.

Leave to cool completely, then dust with cocoa powder. Cut into equal portions and serve.

FLAPJACK PECAN BROWNIES

Two delicious coffeetime treats – the flapjack and the brownie – are combined in this tempting recipe. The base is packed with coconut and pecans and the brownie rich with dark chocolate.

Flapjack base

125 g/1 stick plus 1 tablespoon unsalted butter

100 g/½ cup caster/granulated sugar

100 g/1 scant cup desiccated coconut

100 g/1 cup shelled pecans, finely chopped

Brownie topping

125 g/1 stick plus 1 tablespoon unsalted butter

200 g/7 oz dark/bittersweet chocolate (70% cocoa solids)

125 g/⅔ cup caster/granulated sugar

125 g/½ cup plus 1 tablespoon dark soft brown sugar

3 eggs

1 teaspoon vanilla extract

100 g/1 cup hazelnut flour

a 33 x 23-cm/13 x 9-inch baking pan, greased and lined with baking parchment

Makes 20

Preheat the oven to 190°C (375°F) Gas 5.

To make the flapjack base, put the butter in a saucepan and melt over low heat. Stir in the sugar, coconut and pecans. Mix well so that everything is coated in butter and sugar. Spoon the mixture into the prepared pan and press down evenly with the back of a spoon.

To make the brownie topping, melt the butter and chocolate in a heatproof bowl set over a pan of simmering water. Remove the bowl from the heat and set aside to cool. Put both the sugars, eggs and vanilla extract in a mixing bowl and whisk until the mixture is very light and has doubled in size. Whilst still whisking, slowly pour in the cooled chocolate and butter mixture.

Fold in the hazelnut flour and pour the mixture into the prepared pan. Bake in the preheated oven for about 30–40 minutes, until the topping has formed a crust and a knife inserted in the middle of the brownie comes out clean. Let cool before cutting into squares to serve.

These brownies will keep for up to 5 days if stored in an airtight container.

BONJOUR BROWNIES

This is a classic and delicious recipe with macadamias and walnuts to get you into the brownie spirit. It is very important to cream the butter well, as it will add softness to the brownie while the nuts add some excellent crunch.

240 g/8½ oz. dark/bittersweet chocolate (55% cocoa), chopped

100 g/7 tablespoons unsalted butter, at room temperature and chopped

120 g/generous ½ cup caster/granulated sugar

2 eggs

60 ml/¼ cup milk

120 g/1 scant cup plain/all-purpose flour

25 g/¼ cup ground almonds

1 teaspoon baking powder

1 vanilla pod/bean

20 g/2 tablespoons macadamia nuts

20 g/2 tablespoons walnuts, chopped

a 20-cm/8-inch square baking pan, greased and dusted with flour

Makes 6–8

Preheat the oven to 190°C (375°F) Gas 5.

Put the chocolate in a heatproof bowl set over a saucepan of barely simmering water. Do not let the base of the bowl touch the water. Allow to melt, stirring occasionally, until completely smooth. Remove from the heat.

Put the butter in a bowl and beat with a wooden spoon until very soft. Beat in the sugar until well incorporated, then beat in one egg at a time. Add the milk and stir in. Add the flour, almonds and baking powder and beat in. Split the vanilla pod/bean lengthways and scrape the seeds out into the bowl. Pour the melted chocolate in too and mix everything together well. Finally, stir in the macadamias and walnuts.

Spoon the mixture into the prepared baking pan, spread level with a spatula and bake in the preheated oven for about 20 minutes. Allow the brownies to cool in the pan for a few minutes, then turn out onto a wire rack to cool completely.

Serve at room temperature, cut into equal portions.

ROCKY ROAD FUDGE BARS

This bar cookie is the ultimate Americana, but by incorporating a shortbread base, it has that British touch as well. The best beverage to accompany a Rocky Road Fudge Bar? Coffee, of course.

Shortbread base
120 g/⅔ cup caster/superfine sugar
500 g/4¼ sticks unsalted butter, slightly softened
500 g/3½ cups plain/all-purpose flour
a pinch of salt

Fudge filling
150 g/1¼ sticks unsalted butter
100 g/⅓ cup golden syrup
150 ml/⅔ cup whipping cream
150 g/5½ oz. high-quality dark/bittersweet chocolate, chopped into chunks
500 g/2½ cups caster/superfine sugar
1 teaspoon vanilla extract
80 g/⅔ cup roasted blanched almonds
12 large vanilla marshmallows, chopped into 1.5-cm/½-inch cubes

a baking pan, 30 x 20 x 5-cm/ 12 x 8 x 2 inches, greased and lined with baking parchment

sugar thermometer

Makes 24

Preheat the oven to 170°C (340°F) Gas 4.

To make the shortbread base, beat the sugar and butter until well combined. Fold in the flour and salt until just combined. Transfer the mixture to the prepared brownie pan and pat the dough down until well combined and level. Refrigerate for 5 minutes.

Bake in the preheated oven for 18–25 minutes until the top is golden brown and the edges shrink from the pan edges.

Remove from the oven and let cool.

While the shortbread base is cooling, make the fudge filling. Put the butter, golden syrup, cream, chocolate and sugar into a large saucepan. Add the sugar thermometer and cook over medium heat until the temperature on the thermometer reaches 100°C/212°F. Stir occasionally.

When the mixture looks homogeneous, brush the inside of the saucepan with clean water to dislodge any stray grains of sugar. Keep cooking over medium heat to bring to soft ball stage, 120°C/248°F.

When the fudge reaches 120°C/248°F, remove from the heat and pour into a large, metal mixing bowl. Stir in the vanilla extract and continue stirring until the fudge cools down and loses its glossiness. This can take a few minutes. While still warm and pourable, pour the fudge on top of the shortbread base and let sit for 4 minutes. Before it completely sets, sprinkle the almonds and marshmallows on top and press in slightly. Let cool completely. When cool, remove from the pan and cut into 24 small or 12 large squares.

COFFEE BLONDIES

Use a vegetable peeler to make piles of chocolate shavings for decorating these cappuccino-like squares.

100 g/1 cup shelled pecans
200 g/1 cup light
    muscovado/light brown sugar
175 g/1½ sticks unsalted butter
3 tablespoons instant coffee
    granules
2 eggs, lightly beaten
1 tablespoon pure vanilla extract
250 g/2 cups plain/all-purpose
    flour
2 teaspoons baking powder
a pinch of salt
100 g/⅔ cup dark/bittersweet
    chocolate chips to decorate
200 ml/¾ cup double/heavy
    cream
2 tablespoons icing/
    confectioners' sugar
mixed chocolate shavings
chocolate-coated coffee beans

*a 20 x 30-cm/8 x 12-inch baking
    pan, greased and lined with
    baking parchment*

Makes 16–20

Preheat the oven to 170°C (325°F) Gas 3.

Tip the pecans onto a baking sheet and lightly toast in the preheated oven for 5 minutes. Roughly chop and leave to cool. Leave the oven on for the brownies.

Tip the muscovado/ brown sugar and butter into a medium saucepan over low– medium heat and melt, stirring constantly. In a small bowl, dissolve the coffee granules in 1½ tablespoons boiling water. Stir two-thirds into the pan (reserve the rest for the frosting). Remove from the heat, transfer the mixture to a bowl and leave to cool completely.

Stir the eggs and vanilla extract into the pan until smooth. Sift the flour, baking powder and salt into the pan and fold in until well mixed, then stir in the chocolate chips and pecans. Pour the mixture into the prepared baking pan, spread level and bake on the middle shelf of the preheated oven for about 25 minutes, or until just set in the middle and the top has formed a light crust. Remove from the oven and leave to cool completely in the pan. To decorate, whip the cream with the reserved coffee and sugar. Remove the brownies from the pan, cut into portions, top with a dollop of coffee cream and scatter chocolate shavings and coffee beans over the top.

CARAMEL SHORTBREAD

Caramel or millionaire's shortbread is always popular – a buttery cookie base with a layer of rich, gooey caramel topped with milk/semisweet chocolate. You can replace the milk chocolate topping with dark or white chocolate if you prefer and decorate with sprinkles for a pretty party effect.

Shortbread base

115 g/1 stick unsalted butter, softened

60 g/⅓ cup caster/granulated sugar

85 g gluten-free self-raising/ rising flour OR ¾ cup gluten-free plain/all-purpose baking flour plus 1 teaspoon baking powder and ⅛ teaspoon xanthan gum

85 g/1 cup ground almonds

Caramel layer

60 g/⅓ cup caster/granulated sugar

60 g/½ stick unsalted butter

300 g/1 cup condensed milk

1 teaspoon vanilla extract

Chocolate topping

150 g/5½ oz. milk/semisweet chocolate

a 20-cm/8-inch square baking pan, greased and lined with baking parchment (base and sides)

Makes 16

Preheat the oven to 180°C (350°F) Gas 4.

To make the shortbread base, put the butter and sugar in a mixing bowl and cream together. Sift in the flour then add the almonds and bring the mixture together with your hands to form a soft dough. Press into the prepared pan and prick all over with a fork. Bake in the preheated oven for 15–20 minutes, until the shortbread is golden brown. Let cool in the pan.

Put the sugar, butter, condensed milk and vanilla extract in a small saucepan and warm over gentle heat until the butter has melted and the sugar dissolved. Bring to the boil, beating all the time so that the mixture doesn't stick, then reduce the heat and simmer for about 5 minutes, until golden brown and thick. Pour over the shortbread base and let cool.

To make the chocolate topping, put the chocolate in a heatproof bowl set over a saucepan of barely simmering water and stir gently until melted. Pour the chocolate over the caramel and leave to set. Use a hot knife to cut into 16 squares to serve.

These shortbreads will keep for up to 5 days if stored in an airtight container.

APPLE, FIG AND NUT BARS

Bars could be described as a bake that falls somewhere between a tart and soft cookie. This filling is slightly reminiscent of fig roll but the apples make it lighter. Good for brunch, coffee time or cake sales, or serve warm for dessert.

2 large tart apples, such as
  Granny Smith, peeled, cored
  and finely chopped
2 tablespoons runny honey
2 tablespoons fresh orange juice
2 tablespoons apple juice
  or water
250 g/1½ cups dried figs, finely
  chopped
375 g/2½ cups plain/all-purpose
  flour
145 g/1 cup light brown sugar
250 g/2 sticks plus 2
  tablespoons unsalted butter,
  diced
a good pinch of fine sea salt
½ teaspoon ground cinnamon
125 g/1 cup pecans, hazelnuts,
  walnuts or almonds, finely
  chopped

*a rectangular glass or ceramic
  baking dish, 33 x 23 cm/
  13 x 9 inches, greased*

Makes 16

Preheat the oven to 190°C (375°F) Gas 5.

In a large saucepan, combine the apples, honey, orange and apple juices. Set over low heat, cover and simmer gently, stirring occasionally, until tender, about 10–15 minutes. Use a wooden spoon to help mash the apple pieces. Add the figs and continue simmering, uncovered, until the figs are soft, about 5 minutes. If necessary, add more apple juice or water if the mixture seems too thick, and use a wooden spoon to mash to a coarse purée. Remove from the heat and set aside to cool.

In a food processor, combine the flour, sugar, butter, salt and cinnamon. Pulse to obtain coarse crumbs. Alternatively, blend in a bowl with a pastry cutter, if you have one, or use a palette knife, then rub in using your fingers to obtain coarse crumbs.

Press half the flour mixture into the bottom of the prepared baking dish. Spread the apple and fig mixture over the top in an even layer. Add the nuts to the remaining flour mixture and, using your fingertips, crumble the mixture over the apples in an even layer.

Bake in the preheated oven until browned, about 30–40 minutes. Let cool in the baking dish, then cut into bars. The bars will keep in an airtight container for 7–10 days.

BAKEWELL SLICES

If you like Bakewell tart but have only ever eaten the commercially produced variety, you're in for a treat – this version has a sweet pastry base, good raspberry jam and fragrant frangipane paste topped with almonds.

Pâte sablée

200 g/1½ cups plus
    2 tablespoons plain/all-
    purpose flour
50 g/⅓ cup ground almonds
75 g/⅓ cup caster/granulated
    sugar
160 g/1 stick plus 3 tablespoons
    salted butter, at room
    temperature, cubed
1 egg yolk
150 g/⅔ cup raspberry jam/jelly

Filling

130 g/1 stick plus 1 tablespoon
    salted butter, soft
160 g/¾ cup caster/granulated
    sugar
4 eggs
260 g/1¾ cups ground almonds
40 g/⅓ cup flaked/slivered
    almonds, to decorate

*a 34 x 20 x 3-cm/14 x 8 x 1¼-inch
    baking pan*

baking parchment

baking beans

Makes 12

To make the pâte sablée, put the flour, ground almonds and sugar in a large bowl and stir until evenly mixed. Add the butter and use your fingertips to rub it into the mixture until the texture resembles breadcrumbs. Add the egg yolk and, still using your hands, mix and knead until the dough binds together into a tight, smooth ball – it can seem like it will never bind, but it will!

Wrap the dough in clingfilm/plastic wrap and refrigerate for about 30 minutes until firm.

Preheat the oven to 170°C (325°F) Gas 3.

Remove the pâte sablée from the refrigerator and allow to rest at room temperature for 15 minutes before using.

On a lightly floured work surface, carefully roll out the pâte sablée until about 5 mm/¼ inch thick and use it to line the baking pan. Gently press along the sides and into the corners and trim off the excess pastry with a sharp knife. Prick the base in a few places with a fork and line the tart case with a sheet of baking parchment. Fill the tart case with baking beans and bake blind in the preheated oven for 15–20 minutes. Remove from the oven and set aside to cool. Leave the oven on.

Spread the raspberry jam/jelly evenly over the cooled pastry base. To make the filling, cream together the butter and sugar in a large bowl until pale and fluffy. Add the eggs one at a time, beating after each addition. Add the ground almonds and whisk thoroughly. Spoon the filling over the jam/jelly base and spread to the sides of the pan. Sprinkle the almonds over the top and bake in the hot oven for 30–35 minutes. Remove from the oven and allow to cool before cutting into 12 slices.

CHOCOLATE, GINGER & ORANGE SLICES

These slices have a dense, fudge-like texture – the orange and ginger flavours complement chocolate beautifully.

3 eggs

220 g/1 cup plus 2 tablespoons caster/granulated sugar

300 g/10 oz. dark/bittersweet chocolate, broken into pieces

220 g/scant 2 sticks salted butter

4½ teaspoons vanilla extract

1 tablespoon instant coffee granules

2 tablespoons water, boiling

finely grated zest of 3 oranges

2 nuggets of stem ginger in syrup, drained and finely chopped

2 teaspoons ground ginger

80 g/⅔ cup self-raising/rising flour

50 g/⅓ cup crystallized ginger, finely diced

a 34 x 20 x 3-cm/14 x 8 x 1¼-inch baking pan, greased and lined with baking parchment

Makes 14–16

Preheat the oven to 180°C (350°F) Gas 4.

Put the eggs and sugar in a large bowl. With a balloon whisk or an electric hand whisk, whisk together until smooth, very thick and pale, and no sugar is left in the base of the bowl.

Melt the chocolate and butter in a heatproof bowl set over a pan of simmering water. Do not let the base of the bowl touch the water. Stir frequently until smooth and well mixed. Put the vanilla extract and coffee granules in a cup, add the boiling water and stir vigorously until dissolved and smooth. Add the melted chocolate and butter to the beaten egg and sugar mix, followed by the coffee infusion and the orange zest. Stir with a balloon whisk until smooth. Stir in the stem ginger. Sift together the ground ginger and flour, then gently stir into the bowl until well mixed. Spoon the mixture into the prepared baking pan, sprinkle the crystallized ginger evenly over the top and bake in the preheated oven for 35–40 minutes or until just firm to the touch.

Remove the brownies from the oven and let cool in the pan, then turn out onto a wire rack. They are best eaten warm or at room temperature but are easier to slice when chilled. To portion, refrigerate the brownies until chilled, then slice with a sharp knife. The brownies will keep in an airtight container at room temperature for 7–10 days.

CHOCOLATE TIFFIN

A firm favourite with children, tiffin is a simple, fun-to-make recipe that they'll enjoy helping you with. Using good-quality chocolate, fruit and nuts means this delicious, no-bake cake is equally appealing to adults. Quick and easy to prepare, it is ideal to serve at the end of a family brunch.

400 g/14 oz. digestive biscuits/graham crackers

100 g/⅔ cup sultanas/golden raisins

70 g/½ cup roughly chopped pecans

60 g/½ cup chopped glacé cherries

70 g/½ cup dark/bittersweet chocolate chips or chunks

250 g/8½ oz. dark/bittersweet chocolate, roughly chopped

90 g/⅓ cup plus 1 tablespoon golden syrup

70 g/4½ tablespoons unsalted butter

a 34 x 20 x 3-cm/14 x 8 x 1¼-inch baking pan, greased and lined with baking parchment

Makes 18

Put the biscuits/crackers in a plastic bag and tap them with a rolling pin to break them into small pieces, not crumbs. Put the pieces in a large bowl with the sultanas/golden raisins, pecans, cherries and chocolate chips and mix together with a spoon.

Put the chopped chocolate in a heatproof bowl set over a pan of barely simmering water. Do not let the base of the bowl touch the water. Add the syrup and butter and mix together, stirring continuously, until melted and smooth. This can also be done in a microwave: heat for a few seconds, remove, stir and return to the microwave, repeating until fully melted.

Pour the melted chocolate mixture into the mixing bowl with the dry ingredients and mix until everything is well coated in chocolate.

Spoon the mixture into the prepared baking pan, spread level and press down firmly with the back of the spoon. Refrigerate and allow to harden completely, preferably overnight. To portion, slice using a sharp knife.

The tiffin will keep for 3–5 days in the refrigerator, or freeze for up to 2 months.

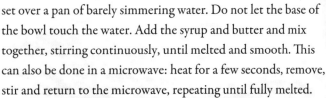

CHOCOLATE FUDGE RASPBERRY SHORTBREAD BARS

This is a sophisticated, bite-size number; the tart fruitiness of the raspberries complements the dark/bittersweet chocolate.

125 g/1 stick unsalted butter, softened

50 g/¼ cup caster/granulated sugar

150 g/1 generous cup plain/all-purpose flour

Chocolate topping

400 ml/1¾ cups double/heavy cream

2 tablespoons icing/confectioners' sugar

400 g/14 oz. dark/bittersweet chocolate (70% cocoa solids), chopped

200 g/1½ cups raspberries

a 20-cm/8-inch square pan, ideally loose-based, greased

Makes 20

Preheat the oven to 190°C (375°F) Gas 5.

Put the butter and sugar in an electric mixer and beat for 3–4 minutes, or until pale and creamy. Tip in the flour and mix again for a few minutes to combine – the dough probably won't come together in a ball, but if you work it briefly with a wooden spoon and then your hands, it will come together. Tip into the prepared pan and press down firmly with the back of a spoon to make an even layer. Prick the base a few times with a fork. Bake in the preheated oven for 20 minutes, or until lightly golden. Let cool.

To make the chocolate topping, bring the cream and icing/confectioners' sugar slowly to the boil in a pan. Put the chocolate in a heatproof bowl. As soon as the cream begins to bubble, remove from the heat and pour into the bowl with the chocolate. Gently whisk together until the chocolate has melted and the mixture is smooth.

Stir the raspberries into the chocolate mixture, then pour it over the cooled crust in the square pan. Let cool completely, then refrigerate for 3 hours, or until set.

Cut into 20 bars with a sharp knife.

STICKY TOFFEE BARS WITH TOFFEE FUDGE DRIZZLE

Try replacing the ginger with 50 g/⅓ cup sultanas/golden raisins in the mix and use golden syrup or maple syrup in the icing instead of the ginger syrup.

175 g/1½ sticks unsalted butter, softened

125 g/½ cup dark muscovado or dark brown sugar

150 g/⅔ cup golden syrup

75 g/⅓ cup black treacle/blackstrap molasses

200 g/1½ cups self-raising/rising flour

1 teaspoon vanilla extract

3 eggs

2 tablespoons double/heavy cream

2 balls stem ginger in syrup, drained and finely chopped

Toffee fudge icing

50 g/3 tablespoons butter

1 tablespoon of the syrup from the jar of stem ginger

2 tablespoons double/heavy cream

75 g/⅓ cup dark muscovado or packed dark brown soft sugar

40 g/⅓ cup icing/confectioners' sugar

a 20 x 33 x 3–4-cm/8 x 13 x 1½-inch baking pan, greased and lined with baking parchment

Makes 14

Preheat the oven to 180°C (350°F) Gas 4.

Put the butter, sugar, golden syrup, treacle/molasses, flour, vanilla extract, eggs and cream in an electric mixer (or use a large mixing bowl and an electric whisk) and beat until combined. Stir in the stem ginger.

Tip the mixture into the prepared pan and spread it evenly with a spatula. Bake in the preheated oven for 25–30 minutes, or until risen and just set in the middle. Let cool completely in the pan.

To make the toffee fudge icing, put the butter, ginger syrup, cream and muscovado sugar in a medium pan over low heat and leave until the butter has melted and the sugar dissolved. Remove the pan from the heat, sift in the icing/confectioners' sugar, then whisk it in.

Remove the cake from the pan and drizzle the icing over it. Let set before cutting into 14 bars.

NO-BAKE CHOCOLATE, MACADAMIA AND FIG SLICES

These are as simple as can be and delicious with an espresso on the side. If you want to make them less sophisticated and more child-friendly, you can replace the macadamia nuts with any other type of nut and the dried figs with raisins or dried apricots.

100 g/6½ tablespoons unsalted butter

2 tablespoons (runny) honey

300 g/10 oz. dark/bittersweet chocolate (50–70% cocoa solids), broken into pieces

100 g/3½ oz. milk/semisweet chocolate, broken into pieces

100 g digestive or other sweetmeal biscuits/6 graham crackers

100 g/⅔ cup shelled macadamia nuts

100 g/⅔ cup ready-to-eat dried figs

cocoa powder, for dusting

an 18-cm/7-inch square pan, ideally loose-based, greased

Makes 16

Put the butter, honey and both types of chocolate in a medium pan and melt gently, stirring from time to time.

Meanwhile, roughly chop the biscuits/crackers, nuts and figs. Stir into the melted chocolate mixture. Tip the mixture into the prepared pan. Let cool completely before refrigerating for 2–3 hours to set.

Dust with cocoa powder and cut into 16 slices.

HONEY, TOASTED PINE NUT AND PUMPKIN SEED FLAPJACKS WITH CHOCOLATE TOPPING

Vary the dried fruit you use in these flapjacks according to what you have handy. They are a hit with children and adults alike.

3 tablespoons pine nuts

2 tablespoons pumpkin seeds

175 g/1½ sticks unsalted butter

100 g/½ cup packed light brown soft sugar

3 tablespoons (runny) honey

100 g/⅔ cup dried sour cherries or cranberries, or chopped ready-to-eat dried apricots, pears, peaches or prunes, or a mixture

250 g/2 cups porridge oats

a pinch of salt

200 g/6½ oz. milk/semisweet chocolate, broken into pieces

a 20-cm/8-inch square, loose-based pan, lightly buttered

Makes 24

Preheat the oven to 180°C (350°F) Gas 4.

Spread the pine nuts and pumpkin seeds on a baking sheet and toast in the preheated oven for 5 minutes, or until lightly golden. Let cool, then roughly chop.

Gently heat the butter, sugar and honey together in a small pan until melted, stirring every now and then. Remove the pan from the heat and let cool slightly.

Tip the dried fruit and oats into a large mixing bowl.

Add the salt and the chopped pine nuts and seeds. Pour in the warm butter mixture and mix well.

Tip the mixture into the prepared pan and press down firmly with the back of a spoon to make an even layer. Put the pan on a baking sheet. Bake in the preheated oven for 30 minutes, or until lightly golden.

Meanwhile, melt the chocolate in a heatproof bowl set over a pan of barely simmering water. Pour over the flapjack, then let cool completely.

Remove the flapjack from the pan and cut into 24 bars.

Chapter 3

DOUGHNUTS, BUNS & ROLLS

COFFEE CREAM DOUGHNUTS

A coffee cream doughnut is one of life's little treats – a caffeine hit and sugar rush all in one go! A perfect morning pick-me-up served with coffee.

200 ml/¾ cup milk, warm

7 g/¼ oz. fast-action dried yeast

30 g/2½ tablespoons caster/
   granulated sugar

300 g/2⅓ cups plain/all-purpose
   flour, plus extra for dusting

160 g/1¼ cups strong white
   bread flour

½ teaspoon salt

2 eggs, beaten

60 g/4 tablespoons unsalted
   butter, softened

sunflower oil, for greasing and frying

Pastry cream

1 tablespoon cornflour/starch

60 g/5 tablespoons caster/
   granulated sugar

1 egg plus 1 egg yolk

100 ml/6½ tablespoons milk

150 ml/⅔ cup double/heavy cream

1 tablespoon instant coffee
   granules

Frosting

350 g/2½ cups icing/
   confectioners' sugar, sifted

2 tablespoons instant coffee
   granules dissolved in 3–4
   tablespoons hot water

20 chocolate coffee beans

20 squares of baking parchment

a piping bag with a round nozzle/tip

Makes 20

For the pastry cream, in a mixing bowl whisk the cornflour/starch, sugar, whole egg and egg yolk until creamy. Put the milk, cream and coffee granules in a pan set over gentle heat and warm, stirring until the coffee has dissolved, then bring to a boil. Slowly pour over the egg mixture, whisking all the time. Return the mixture to the pan and cook for a few minutes until thick, then pass through a sieve/strainer to remove any lumps. Let cool then chill.

To make the doughnuts see page 95, second paragraph (omitting the lemon zest).

Lay the squares of baking parchment on a tray and dust with flour. Divide the dough into 20 portions and, dusting your hands with flour, shape each one into a ball and place on a square of baking parchment. Cover with a clean damp kitchen towel and let rest for 10 minutes. Reshape the balls and then let rise in a warm place for 35–45 minutes, covered in lightly-greased clingfilm/plastic wrap, until the dough has doubled in size and holds an indent when you press with a fingertip. Rest again, uncovered, for 10 minutes.

To cook the doughnuts, in a large saucepan or deep fat fryer, heat the oil to 190°C (375°F). Holding the square of parchment, transfer each doughnut to the pan, one at a time, being careful not to handle the dough or splash hot oil. Cook in small batches for about 1½ minutes on each side until golden brown. Remove from the oil using a slotted spoon and drain on paper towels.

When the doughnuts are cool, use a round teaspoon handle to poke a hole in the doughnut and make a cavity inside. Spoon the pastry cream into a piping bag and pipe into the doughnuts. For the frosting, put the icing/confectioners' sugar in a bowl and add the coffee gradually, stirring until you have a thick, frosting. Spread over the top of each doughnut and decorate with a bean.

CARAMEL RING DOUGHNUTS

These fudge flavoured doughnuts are delicious and light as they are baked rather than fried. Topped with a buttery toffee glaze and fudge pieces, they are a caramel-lover's dream.

300 g/2⅓ cups self-raising/rising flour
1 teaspoon baking powder
85 g/scant ½ cup soft light brown sugar
½ teaspoon salt
2 eggs, beaten
50 g/3 tablespoons unsalted butter, softened
125 ml/½ cup milk
125 ml/½ cup plain yogurt
1 teaspoon vanilla extract
80 g/3½ oz. fudge, cut into small pieces, to decorate

Caramel glaze

60 g/4 tablespoons unsalted butter
115 g/½ cup plus 1 tablespoon soft light brown sugar
160 ml/⅔ cup milk
440 g/3 cups icing/confectioners' sugar, sifted

3 x 6-hole doughnut pans, greased

Makes 18

Preheat the oven to 350°F (180°C) Gas 4.

Sift the flour into a large mixing bowl. Add all the remaining doughnut ingredients (except the fudge pieces) and beat to a smooth batter with a stand mixer or electric hand whisk.

Spoon the mixture into the prepared doughnut pans. Bake in the preheated oven for 10–15 minutes until the doughnuts are golden brown. If you don't have three doughnut pans, you can bake them in batches, washing the pan between each batch. Remove from the oven and turn the doughnuts out onto a wire rack to cool. Slide a sheet of foil under the rack to catch any drips of glaze.

For the caramel glaze, put the butter and sugar in a small saucepan and heat gently until the sugar has dissolved. Remove the pan from the heat, let cool slightly and then add the milk and return to the heat, stirring until well combined. Add the icing/confectioners' sugar and beat over the heat until you have a smooth toffee glaze. Remove the pan from the heat and, one at a time, dip each doughnut in the glaze to coat completely. Remove with a slotted spoon and transfer to a wire rack, then sprinkle over the fudge pieces whilst the glaze is still sticky (it is best to do this in batches). Leave to set before serving.

PISTACHIO TRIANGLE DOUGHNUTS

These doughnuts may look classic from the outside but inside they are bursting with a delicious pistachio cream. Roll in pistachio sugar for a pretty effect.

200 ml/¾ cup milk, warm

7 g/¼ oz. fast-action dried yeast

30 g/2½ tablespoons caster/
   granulated sugar

300 g/2⅓ cups plain/all-purpose
   flour, plus extra for dusting

160 g/1¼ cups strong white
   bread flour

½ teaspoon salt

2 eggs, beaten

60 g/4 tablespoons unsalted
   butter, softened

60 g/½ cup shelled and finely
   chopped pistachios

sunflower oil, for greasing and
   frying

Pistachio cream

30 g/2 tablespoons butter

60 g/½ cup shelled pistachios

60 g/½ cup icing/confectioners'
   sugar, sifted

300 ml/1¼ cups double/heavy
   cream

Pistachio sugar

60 g/½ cup shelled pistachios

150 g/¾ cup caster/superfine
   sugar

26 squares of baking parchment

4-cm/1½-inch triangular cutter

*a piping bag with a round
   nozzle/tip*

Makes 26

For the doughnuts, whisk together the warm milk, yeast and sugar in a jug/pitcher and leave in a warm place for about 10 minutes until a thick foam has formed on top of the milk. Meanwhile, sift the flours into a large mixing bowl, add the salt, eggs, butter and chopped pistachios and stir together, then pour in the yeast mixture. Using a stand mixer fitted with a dough hook, mix the dough on a slow speed for 2 minutes, then increase the speed and knead for about 8 minutes until the dough is soft and pliable. Alternatively, knead the dough by hand for 15 minutes. The dough will be very soft but not sticky, so dust with flour if needed.

Lay the squares of baking parchment on a tray and dust with flour. Roll out the dough to 3 cm/1¼ inch thickness and cut out 26 triangles, re-modelling the dough scraps if necessary. Place each triangle on a square of baking parchment. Cover the doughnuts with a clean damp kitchen towel and let rest for 10 minutes. Reshape the triangles and then let rise in a warm place for about 35–45 minutes, covered in lightly-greased clingfilm/plastic wrap, until they have doubled in size and hold an indent when you press with a fingertip. Rest again, uncovered, for 10 minutes.

To cook the doughnuts see page 84, fourth paragraph.

To make the pistachio sugar, blitz the pistachios to a fine dust in a food processor. Add the sugar, blend again briefly to combine and then transfer to a shallow dish. While still warm, roll each doughnut in pistachio sugar to coat. Use a round teaspoon handle to poke a hole in the doughnut and make a cavity inside.

For the pistachio cream, blitz the butter, pistachios and sugar to a smooth paste in a food processor. Whip the cream until it almost holds stiff peaks then add the pistachio paste and whisk again until the cream is stiff. Pipe the cream into each doughnut.

BOMBOLINI

The Bombolini is a light dough filled with a chocolate nougatine cream and this is a take on the Italian recipe – truly delicious!

200 ml/¾ cup milk, warm

7 g/¼ oz. fast-action dried yeast

30 g/2½ tablespoons caster/
  granulated sugar

300 g/2⅓ cups plain/all-purpose
  flour, plus extra for dusting

170 g/1⅓ cups strong white
  bread flour

½ teaspoon salt

2 eggs, beaten

60 g/4 tablespoons unsalted
  butter, softened

1 tablespoon hazelnut butter

sunflower oil, for greasing and
  frying

100 g/3½ oz. milk/semisweet
  chocolate, melted

50 g/⅓ cup toasted hazelnuts,
  chopped

Cream filling

270 g/1 generous cup chocolate
  hazelnut spread (such as
  Nutella), at room temperature

200 ml/¾ cup crème fraîche

1 generous tablespoon hazelnut
  butter

*32 small squares of baking
  parchment*

*a piping bag with a round
  nozzle/tip*

Makes 32

Whisk together the warm milk, yeast and sugar in a jug/pitcher and leave in a warm place for about 10 minutes until a thick foam has formed on top of the milk. Meanwhile, sift the flours into a large mixing bowl, add the salt, eggs, butter and hazelnut butter and stir together, then pour in the yeast mixture. Using a stand mixer fitted with a dough hook, mix the dough on a slow speed for 2 minutes, then increase the speed and knead for about 8 minutes until the dough is soft and pliable. Alternatively, knead the dough by hand for 15 minutes. The mixture will be very soft but should not be sticky, so dust with flour if needed.

Lay the squares of baking parchment on a tray and lightly dust with flour. Divide the dough into 32 portions and, dusting your hands with flour, shape each portion into a ball and place on a square of baking parchment. Cover the doughnuts with a clean damp kitchen towel and leave to rest for 10 minutes. Reshape the balls and then let rise in a warm place for about 35–45 minutes, covered in lightly-greased clingfilm/plastic wrap, until the dough has doubled in size and holds an indent when you press with a fingertip. Rest again, uncovered, for 10 minutes.

To cook the doughnuts see page 84, fourth paragraph.

When cool enough to handle, use a round teaspoon handle to poke a hole in the doughnut and move it around to make a cavity inside.

For the cream filling, beat together the chocolate hazelnut spread, crème fraîche and hazelnut butter until creamy. Spoon the cream into a piping bag and pipe into the cavity in each doughnut. To decorate, drizzle the doughnuts with the melted chocolate and sprinkle over the toasted hazelnuts.

CRUELLERS

Cruellers are light doughnuts made with either a cake or choux batter and piped into elegant star rings. To ensure that the doughnuts hold their shape you need to chill them in the freezer for a short while before frying.

300 g/3⅓ cups self-raising/rising
    flour, plus extra for dusting
1 teaspoon baking powder
70 g/⅓ cup caster/granulated
    sugar
¼ teaspoon salt
2 eggs, beaten
50 g/3 tablespoons unsalted
    butter, softened
1 teaspoon vanilla extract
250 ml/1 cup plain yogurt
sunflower oil, for frying

Glaze
freshly squeezed juice of
    2–3 lemons
250 g/2 cups icing/
    confectioners' sugar, sifted

2 baking sheets (small enough
    to fit in your freezer), lined with
    baking parchment

a piping bag with a large star
    nozzle/tip

Makes 16

Sift the flour into a large mixing bowl. Add all the remaining ingredients (except the frying oil) and beat to a smooth batter with an electric hand whisk. Spoon the mixture into the piping bag. Dust the prepared baking sheet with flour and pipe circles of dough onto the sheet about 8 cm/3 inches in diameter. Put the baking sheet in the freezer to chill for 10 minutes.

Fill a large saucepan or deep fat fryer 10 cm/4 inches deep with oil and heat it to 190°C (375°F). Gently remove the cruellers from the parchment and transfer to the pan, a few at a time, being careful not to splash hot oil. Cook on each side for about 2 minutes until golden brown. Remove one crueller from the oil and cut it open to ensure the cake dough is cooked all the way through. When satisfied they are cooked, remove the doughnuts from the oil using a slotted spoon, drain on paper towels and let cool on a wire rack. Slide a sheet of foil under the rack to catch any drips of glaze.

For the dipping glaze, put the lemon juice and icing/confectioners' sugar in a saucepan set over medium heat, stir and simmer for 3–5 minutes until syrupy. For a thin syrup coating use the juice of 3 lemons or for a white frosting use 2. Drizzle the lemon glaze over the cruellers and leave to set before serving.

AUSTRIAN APRICOT DOUGHNUTS

These delicious Krapfen – doughnuts filled with apricot jam and dusted with icing sugar – are traditionally served in Austria at Carnival time. You can serve any left-over purée alongside the doughnuts for dipping.

200 ml/¾ cup milk, warm

7 g/¼ oz. fast-action dried yeast

30 g/2½ tablespoons caster/
    granulated sugar

300 g/2⅓ cups plain/all-purpose
    flour, plus extra for dusting

160 g/1¼ cups strong white
    bread flour

½ teaspoon salt

2 eggs, beaten

60 g/4 tablespoons unsalted
    butter, softened

grated zest of 2 lemons

sunflower oil, for greasing and
    frying

icing/confectioners' sugar, for
    dusting

Apricot filling

8 ripe fresh apricots, pitted and
    chopped

130 g/⅔ cup caster/granulated
    sugar

freshly squeezed juice of 1 large
    lemon

1 teaspoon vanilla extract

16 small squares of baking
    parchment

a piping bag with a round
    nozzle/tip

Makes 16

To make the apricot filling, put the chopped apricots in a saucepan with the sugar, lemon juice and vanilla and simmer until the fruit is soft. Purée in a food processor and set aside to cool.

To make the doughnuts, whisk together the warm milk, yeast and sugar in a jug/pitcher and leave in a warm place for 10 minutes until a thick foam has formed on top of the milk. Meanwhile, sift the flours into a large mixing bowl, add the salt, eggs, butter and lemon zest and stir together, then pour in the yeast mixture. Using a stand mixer fitted with a dough hook, mix the dough on a slow speed for 2 minutes, then increase the speed and knead for about 8 minutes until the dough is soft and pliable. Alternatively, knead the dough by hand for 15 minutes. The mixture will be very soft but should not be sticky, so dust with flour if needed.

Lay the squares of baking parchment on a tray and lightly dust with flour. Divide the dough into 16 portions and, dusting your hands with flour, shape each portion into a ball and place on a square of baking parchment. Cover with a damp kitchen towel and let rest for 10 minutes. Reshape the balls and let rise in a warm place for 35–45 minutes, covered in lightly-greased clingfilm/plastic wrap, until the dough has doubled in size and holds an indent when you press with a fingertip. Rest again, uncovered, for 10 minutes.

To cook the doughnuts, see fourth paragraph page 84.

When cool enough to handle, use a round teaspoon handle to poke a hole in the doughnut and make a cavity inside. Spoon the apricot purée into the piping bag and pipe it into the cavity in each doughnut. Dust with icing/confectioners' sugar to serve.

RICOTTA DOUGHNUTS

Zeppole are irresistible light ricotta doughnuts that are a snip to make at home. They are wonderful served warm straight from the pan, with a snowy shower of icing sugar. The singular is zeppola, but just try to resist a second or third!

100 g/¾ cup plus 1 tablespoon
    plain/all-purpose flour
2 teaspoons baking powder
a pinch of salt
30 g/3 tablespoons
    caster/granulated sugar
250 g/8 oz. ricotta cheese
2 eggs
sunflower oil, for deep frying
icing/confectioners' sugar, for
    dusting

a deep-fat fryer (optional)

Makes about 12

Sift the flour into a large bowl and add the baking powder, salt and sugar. Beat the ricotta and eggs together until smooth. Stir the ricotta mixture into the dry ingredients until thoroughly combined.

Heat the oil in a large saucepan or deep-fat fryer to 375°F (190°C). Drop several tablespoons of the batter into the hot oil at the same time. Fry the zeppole for 3–4 minutes, turning regularly, until they are puffed, fluffy and golden. Remove from the pan with a slotted spoon and drain on paper towels. Repeat until all the batter is used up. Dust liberally with icing/confectioners' sugar and serve warm.

BOSTON CAKE

This is a festive cake and should be pulled apart and enjoyed individually while still warm. As for why this is called a Boston Cake – it's a mystery!

Dough

245 ml/1¼ cups lukewarm milk

75 g/¼ cup caster/granulated
   sugar

25 g/1 cake fresh yeast (or easy-
   blend dried yeast according to
   manufacturer's instructions)

½ teaspoon cardamom seeds,
   crushed

90 g/¾ stick unsalted butter,
   melted

1 egg

500 g/4 cups plain/all-purpose
   flour

Filling

50 g/3½ tablespoons unsalted
   butter, softened at room
   temperature

100 g/½ cup dark brown sugar

1½ tablespoons ground cinnamon

Glaze

45 g/¼ cup caster/superfine
   sugar

½ tablespoon freshly squeezed
   lemon juice

1 egg, lightly beaten, for glazing

caster/superfine sugar, for
   sprinkling

*2 baking sheets, lined with
   baking parchment*

*a 25-cm/10-inch round cake
   pan, greased*

Makes 8–9

To make the dough, put the milk, sugar, yeast, cardamom, melted butter and egg in a food processor or mixer with a dough hook. With the motor running, gradually add the flour until it is all incorporated and the dough has come together. Transfer the dough to a bowl, cover with a clean kitchen towel and leave to prove in a warm place for 1 hour, or until it has doubled in size.

After the first proving, punch down the dough and transfer to a lightly floured work surface. Using a rolling pin, roll it out until it is about 30 x 40 cm/12 x 16 inches and 1 cm/½ inch thick.

For the filling, spread the butter evenly over the dough and sprinkle the sugar and cinnamon all over the top.

Roll the dough up from a long side, then cut into roughly 4-cm/1¾-inch rolls. Arrange the rolls, cut-side down, in the prepared cake pan. They should fit quite snugly.

Preheat the oven to 200°C (400°F) Gas 6.

Cover with the kitchen towel again and leave to prove in a warm place for 15 minutes.

Brush the tops of the buns with the beaten egg and sprinkle with caster/superfine sugar. Bake the cake in the preheated oven for 25 minutes, or until golden brown.

Remove from the oven and leave to cool in the pan for 10 minutes before tipping out onto a wire rack.

ALMOND TWISTS

Instead of ground almonds, you can also use a cinnamon and sugar mix.

250 ml/1 cup milk, lukewarm

1 egg, lightly beaten

85 g/a scant ½ cup caster/granulated sugar

1 teaspoon salt

2 teaspoons cardamom seeds, crushed with a pestle and mortar

7 g/¼ oz. fast-action dried yeast

500 g/4 cups strong white bread flour

75 g/5 tablespoons unsalted butter, softened at room temperature

20 g/¼ cup flaked/slivered almonds

Filling and glaze

25 g/⅓ cup ground almonds

25 g/⅓ cup caster/granulated sugar

50 g/2 tablespoons unsalted butter, softened at room temperature

1 egg, lightly beaten

1–2 baking sheets, lined with baking parchment

Makes 15

Heat the milk in a large saucepan until lukewarm. Whisk the egg with a little of the warm milk, then pour into the pan and whisk. Add the sugar, salt and cardamom to the pan and mix well.

Mix the yeast and flour together, then add a little of the flour mixture to the saucepan and whisk well. Continue to add the flour mixture, first by whisking and then, when the mixture gets too stiff, with a wooden spoon. Finally, add the butter and turn out onto a lightly floured surface to knead the dough with your hands until all the ingredients are thoroughly incorporated.

Transfer the dough to a lightly floured surface and knead for 10 minutes, or until the dough is elastic and no longer sticky. Add a little more flour, if necessary. Return the dough to the bowl, cover with a clean kitchen towel and leave to rise in a warm place for 1 hour, or until doubled in size.

Preheat the oven to 200°C (400°F) Gas 6.

After 1 hour, punch down the dough and knead it on the floured surface again for a few minutes. Using a rolling pin, roll it out until it is about 30 x 50 cm/12 x 20 inches.

To make the filling, mix the almonds and sugar together. Next, spread the butter over the dough. Scatter the almond mixture over one half of the rectangle. Fold the bare pastry half over the filling and press gently together. Place the rectangle, now measuring 30 x 25 cm/12 x 10 inches, horizontally in front of you. Using a sharp knife, cut the pastry into 25-cm/10-inch-long and 2-cm/¾-inch-wide strips. Hold a strip between your fingers and twist in opposite directions, then roughly coil it in on itself and press the ends together underneath. Arrange on the prepared baking sheets, cover with kitchen towels and leave to prove in a warm place for another 10 minutes. Brush the beaten egg over the top and sprinkle with the flaked almonds. Bake in the preheated oven for 10 minutes.

MEXICAN COFFEE BUNS

These buns are sold all over Malaysia and a bakery chain called Rotiboy has made them so famous that they are often called Rotiboy buns.

Scalded dough
100 g/¾ cup plain/all-purpose flour
70 g/⅓ cup boiling water

Dough
400 g/3¼ cups plain/all-purpose
  flour
2.5 g/1¼ teaspoons instant yeast,
  5 g/1¾ teaspoons dry yeast, or
  10 g/0.35 oz fresh yeast
80 g/6 tablespoons caster/
  granulated sugar
175 g/⅔ cup milk, heated up to
  just below boiling point, then
  cooled to room temperature
10 g/2½ teaspoons salt
1 egg
60 g/5 tablespoons unsalted
  butter, cubed

Filling
100 g/6½ tablespoons unsalted
  butter, cubed

Topping
125 g/8 tablespoons butter,
  at room temperature
125 g/1 scant cup icing/
  confectioners' sugar
1 egg
240 g/2 cups plain/all-purpose
  flour

*baking sheets lined with baking
  parchment*
Makes 12

To make the scalded dough, put the flour into a little bowl and pour over the boiling water. Stir with a spoon to mix the flour and water. Cover with clingfilm/plastic wrap and set aside.

To make the dough, put the flour into a big mixing bowl and make a well. Sprinkle the yeast and sugar into the well and then pour over the cooled milk. Flick some flour over the milk to close the well, cover and allow to rest for 1 hour.

Add the salt, egg and cooled scalded dough (break it up into bits as this makes it easier to incorporate it) to the dough and bring the ingredients together in the bowl. Turn the dough out onto the counter and knead well for 10 minutes. Add the butter and knead again for 10 minutes. Put the dough back in the bowl, cover and allow to rest for 2 hours. Pull the dough out onto an unfloured surface.

To shape, divide the dough into 12 equal portions. Roll each portion into a tight ball. Allow to rest under a dry kitchen towel for 15 minutes. Gently flatten each piece of dough with your hands into a disc about 3 cm/1¼ inches in diameter and then place a little cube of butter in the centre. Stretch the dough around the butter, roll it up and shape into a stuffed ball.

Place on the prepared baking sheet. Repeat for the remaining dough. Cover with the dry kitchen towel and let rest for 30 minutes.

Beat together the ingredients for the topping. Pipe a thin swirl on the top of each bun. Allow the buns to rest, uncovered, for about 15 minutes.

Preheat the oven to 220°C (425°F) Gas 7.

Bake in the preheated oven for 15 minutes. Remove from the oven and cool completely on a wire rack before eating.

VIGILANTES

Get this: vigilantes are the snack of choice of the Uruguayan police force! That has got to be reason enough to bake them.

300 g/2⅓ cups plain/all-purpose
    flour
50 g/¼ cup caster/granulated
    sugar
1.5 g/¾ teaspoon instant yeast,
    3 g/1 teaspoon dry yeast,
    or 6 g/0.2 oz. fresh yeast
200 g/¾ cup plus 1 tablespoon
    milk, heated up to just below
    boiling point, then cooled to
    room temperature
6 g/1½ teaspoons salt
50 g/3 tablespoons unsalted
    butter

Filling
red fruit jam/jelly of your choice

Glaze
1 egg, beaten
1 tablespoon water
a pinch of salt
a pinch of sugar

*baking sheets lined with baking
    parchment*

Makes 20

Put the flour into a large bowl and make a well. Sprinkle the sugar and the yeast into the well and pour in the cooled milk. Flick some flour over the milk to close the well and then cover the bowl. Allow to rest for 1 hour.

Add the salt and mix the ingredients together into a ball in the bowl. Turn this out onto the counter and knead for 10 minutes. Add the butter and knead for a further 10 minutes.

Put the dough back into the bowl and cover it. Allow to rest for 2 hours.

Pull the dough out onto an unfloured surface.

Divide the dough into 20 equal portions. Lightly flour the counter. Gently stretch each piece of dough into a little diamond shape and place it on the counter.

Smear a little of the jam/jelly from the top corner to the bottom corner of the dough.

Brush the edges of the dough with water and then fold the right corner over the jam/jelly and fold the left corner over the right corner to the edge of the dough.

Pick this up with a scraper and pop it on a prepared baking sheet, folded-side-up.

Repeat for all the other pieces of dough, making sure you leave some room between each bun. Cover with a dry kitchen towel and allow to rest for 45 minutes.

Preheat the oven to 220°C (425°F) Gas 7.

Beat together the ingredients for the glaze. Brush the glaze over the buns and pop them in the preheated oven. Bake for 15 minutes. Remove from the oven and allow to cool completely on a wire rack before eating them.

CHOCOLATE STICKS

It is hard to resist eating these chocolate sticks warm and they are wonderful dipped into a cup of coffee.

Predough
100 g/scant ½ cup warm water
150 g/1 heaping cup plain/all-purpose flour
a pinch of yeast (any kind will do)

Dough
300 g/2⅓ cups plain/all-purpose flour
50 g/¼ cup caster/granulated sugar
1 g/½ teaspoon instant yeast, 2 g/1 scant teaspoon dry yeast, or 4 g/0.15 oz. fresh yeast
200 g/¾ cup milk, heated up to boiling point, then cooled to room temperature
5 g/1¼ teaspoons salt

Filling
50 g/3 tablespoons unsalted butter, melted and allowed to cool slightly
200 g/6½ oz. dark/bittersweet chocolate chips or chunks

Glaze
1 egg
1 tablespoon water
a pinch of salt
a pinch of sugar

baking sheets lined with baking parchment

Makes 8 (depending on length)

Make the predough a day before you want to bake the buns. Mix together the water, flour and yeast in a bowl until they are well blended. Cover with clingfilm/plastic wrap and allow to sit on the counter for 12–48 hours.

To make the dough, put the flour into a big bowl and make a well. Sprinkle the sugar and yeast into the well and pour in the cooled milk. Flick some flour over the milk to close the well and allow to rest for 1 hour. Add the salt and the predough from the night before. Bring it all together in a ball in the bowl. Pull it out onto the counter and knead well for 10 minutes.

Lightly flour a surface and roll out the dough to a thickness of 5 mm/¼ inch. Brush the top with some of the melted butter for the filling and cover it with clingfilm/plastic wrap. Let rest for 2 hours.

Scatter a third of the chocolate chips over the dough. Fold the left edge to the middle and fold the right edge in to meet it. Flour around the dough. Roll the dough flat again, brush some more melted butter on it and scatter over another third of the chocolate chips. Fold the dough as above and flour around it. Roll the dough flat again, brush some more melted butter on it and scatter over the final third of the chocolate chips. Fold the dough as above, lightly flour it and flip it over so the floury side is down. Flour the top, cover with a kitchen towel and allow to rest for 45 minutes.

Preheat the oven to 230°C (450°F) Gas 8.

Beat together the ingredients for the glaze and brush it over the dough. Using a knife, scraper or pizza cutter, cut the dough into strips about 2.5 cm/1 inch wide.

Place the strips on the prepared baking sheets. Bake in the preheated oven for 15 minutes. Remove from the oven.

MONKEY BUNS

The origin of the name Monkey Buns (also called African Coffee Cake) is uncertain. What is not uncertain is that they are delicious.

600 g/4¾ cups plain/all-purpose
    flour
3 g/1½ teaspoons instant yeast,
6 g/2 teaspoons dry yeast, or
    12 g/0.42 oz. fresh yeast
50 g/¼ cup caster/granulated
    sugar
225 g/1 cup milk, heated up to
    boiling point, then cooled to
    room temperature
12 g/1 tablespoon salt
2 eggs
2 teaspoons vanilla extract
50 g/3 tablespoons unsalted
    butter

Topping

100 g/½ cup brown sugar
2 tablespoons ground cinnamon
100 g/¾ cup chopped pecans
100 g/6½ tablespoons unsalted
    butter

*baking pan with deep sides and
    solid base, buttered*

Makes 24

Put the flour into a large bowl and make a well. Sprinkle the yeast and sugar in the well and pour over the cooled milk. Flick some flour over the surface of the milk to close the well and allow to rest for 1 hour.

Sprinkle the salt around the edge of the flour, add the eggs and vanilla extract into the centre and bring everything together in the bowl. Turn the dough out onto the counter and knead for 10 minutes. Add the butter and knead for a further 10 minutes. Put the dough back in the bowl and allow to rest for 2 hours.

Turn the dough out onto an unfloured surface. It is sticky but try not to add more flour. The stickiness is important, as you will see later on. Divide the dough into 4 equal portions. Shape each portion into a tight sausage. Cut each sausage into 6 pieces and allow to rest under a dry kitchen towel for 15 minutes.

Butter a baking pan with deep sides. The buns will rise, so pick a pan that is big enough so that the buns do not come all the way over the top before they are baked.

Form each portion of dough into a tight ball. Mix the brown sugar and cinnamon together. Put 6 buns in the bottom of the pan and sprinkle a third of the cinnamon sugar and a third of the pecans over the dough. Repeat until you have used up all the dough balls, cinnamon sugar and pecans. Cover and allow to rest for 45 minutes.

Preheat the oven to 200°C (400°F) Gas 6.

Before baking the buns, melt the butter and let it cool slightly. Pour the melted butter evenly over the buns and bake in the preheated oven for 45 minutes. After 30 minutes, cover them with baking parchment so they don't get too brown. Remove from the oven. Allow to rest in the pan for 10 minutes before turning them out onto a plate and sharing them.

AUTUMNAL STICKY BUNS

Sticky buns come in many varieties. This recipe, however, has a twist. Rather than milk or water for the liquid in the dough, you use puréed pumpkin and if you cannot find that, you can use puréed apple or pear.

600 g/4¾ cups plain/all-purpose flour

3 g/1½ teaspoons instant yeast, 6 g/2 teaspoons dry yeast, or 12 g/0.42 oz. fresh yeast

50 g/¼ cup caster/granulated sugar

75 g/scant ⅓ cup milk, heated up to boiling point, then cooled to room temperature

12 g/1 tablespoon salt

1 egg

350 g/scant 1½ cups pumpkin purée

50 g/3 tablespoons unsalted butter

Filling

50 g/3 tablespoons pumpkin purée

1 teaspoon each ground ginger nutmeg, cinnamon and allspice

50 g/¼ cup brown sugar

50 g/3 tablespoons unsalted butter, softened

Goo

100 g/6½ tablespoons unsalted butter, melted

100 g/½ cup brown sugar

75 g/⅓ cup milk or cream

100 g/¾ cup chopped pecans

large, deep roasting pan

Makes 16

Put the flour into a big bowl and make a well. Sprinkle the yeast and sugar into the well and pour over the cooled milk. Flick some flour on the surface of the milk to close the well. Allow to rest for 1 hour.

Sprinkle the salt around the edge of the flour and add the egg and the pumpkin purée. Gather everything into a ball and then turn it out onto the counter. Knead for 10 minutes. Add the butter and knead for another 10 minutes. Pop it back in the bowl and allow it to rest for 2 hours.

Beat together the ingredients for the filling and set aside.

Mix together the ingredients for the goo and pour the mixture into a large, deep roasting pan. Set aside.

Pull the dough out onto a floured surface. Roll the dough with a rolling pin into a rectangle about 40 x 20 cm/ 16 x 8 inches. Spread the filling evenly over the dough and then roll the rectangle up into a tight sausage from the long side. Slice the sausage into 16 equal pieces. Place each piece in the baking pan on top of the goo. Snuggle them together if you have to in order to fit them all in. Cover and allow to rest for 45 minutes.

Preheat the oven to 200°C (400°F) Gas 6.

Put the buns in the preheated oven and bake for 45 minutes. After 30 minutes, cover them with baking parchment or aluminium foil to prevent the tops getting too brown. When they are done, remove from the oven, place a large plate over the pan and carefully invert the buns onto the plate. Don't spill the hot goo! It's delicious and you don't want to waste any or to burn yourself. Allow to cool slightly before eating.

COFFEE AND CINNAMON ROLLS

Warm, spicy cinnamon and smooth, rich coffee work in perfect harmony in these sticky, sweet rolls. They're wonderful eaten warm, fresh from the oven, and make the perfect choice for a leisurely brunch.

400 g/2⅔ cups strong white
   bread flour
2 tablespoons caster/granulated
   sugar
½ teaspoon salt
2 teaspoons fast-action dried
   yeast
3 eggs
80 ml/⅓ cup lukewarm milk
50 g/3 tablespoons unsalted
   butter, melted

Filling
115 g/1 stick butter, at room
   temperature
115 g/⅔ cup soft light brown
   sugar
1 tablespoon ground cinnamon
1½ tablespoons freshly brewed
   espresso

Glaze
40 g/3 tablespoons unsalted
   butter
1–2 tablespoons freshly brewed
   espresso
140 g/1 cup icing/confectioners'
   sugar, sifted

2 large 6-hole muffin pans

Makes 12

Sift the flour, sugar, salt and yeast into a large bowl, combine, then make a well in the centre. Mix together the eggs, milk and butter, then pour into the flour mixture and stir together.

Turn the dough out on to a floured surface and knead for 5–10 minutes, working in a little more flour if necessary, until smooth and elastic. Put in a lightly greased bowl, grease the top of the dough, cover in clingfilm/plastic wrap and leave in a warm place for about 1 hour until doubled in size.

Cut out twelve 15-cm/6-inch squares of baking parchment and use to line the muffin pans. To make the filling, beat together the butter, sugar, cinnamon and espresso. Cover and chill for about 30 minutes.

Turn the dough out on to a floured surface and punch down, then divide into two pieces. Roll out each piece to 20 x 26 cm/8 x 10 inches. Spread the filling over the dough and gently roll up from one long side to form a roll. Slice each roll into six pieces and put in the lined muffin cups. Wrap each muffin pan in a plastic bag and leave in a warm place for 30 minutes until almost doubled in size.

Preheat the oven to 190°C (375°F) Gas 5. Bake the rolls for 15 minutes until risen and golden, then transfer to a wire rack.

While the rolls cool, make the glaze. Put the butter and espresso in a pan and heat gently until the butter has melted. Stir in the sugar and heat gently, stirring, for about 3 minutes until smooth and glossy and just bubbling. Bubble very gently for a further minute, then spoon over the rolls. Serve warm.

SOPAPILLAS

These little doughnuts are popular the world over in variations of this recipe. The classic way to serve them is dusted with icing sugar and drizzled with a little extra honey. Sometimes they are even served in place of bread to accompany soups and casseroles. Whatever the origins of these dainty fried delights, one thing is sure; served warm, they are irresistible.

220 g/1¾ cups self-raising/rising flour, sifted, plus extra for dusting

1 teaspoon baking powder

¼ teaspoon salt

1 teaspoon vanilla extract

1 tablespoon honey, plus extra to serve

50 g/3 tablespoons unsalted butter, softened

sunflower or vegetable oil, for frying

icing/confectioners' sugar, for dusting

Makes about 60

Put the flour, baking powder, salt, vanilla, honey and butter in a large mixing bowl and blend with an electric hand whisk. Gradually add 125 ml/½ cup water until you have a very soft, but not sticky, dough. Wrap the dough in clingfilm/plastic wrap and chill in the fridge for about 30 minutes.

Dust a clean work surface with flour and roll out the dough to ½ cm/¼ inch thick – it is easiest to do this in batches, rolling out a quarter of the dough at a time. Cut the dough into diamond shapes about 5 cm/2 inches in length.

In a large saucepan or deep fat fryer, heat the oil to 190°C (375°F). Add the sopapillas to the pan in batches, being careful not to splash hot oil. Fry for 3 minutes on one side and then turn over and cook them for a further minute on the other, until golden brown all over. Remove them from the oil using a slotted spoon and drain on paper towels.

While still warm, dust the sopapillas with icing/confectioners' sugar. Serve drizzled with a little runny honey. These doughnuts will keep for about 3 days if stored in an airtight container.

Chapter 4

PASTRIES, TARTS & CHEESECAKES

COFFEE RELIGIEUSE

These delicate coffee buns are a firm favourite. With a strong coffee icing and bitter coffee filling they are a great pick-me-up treat.

1 quantity Basic Choux
  Pastry/Paste (see page 7)

Icing

250 g/2 cups fondant icing/
  confectioners' sugar, sifted
45 ml/3 tablespoons espresso
  coffee
12 coffee bean shaped
  chocolates or decorations

Filling

1 tablespoon instant coffee
  granules, dissolved in 2
  tablespoons just-boiled water
350 ml/1½ cups double/heavy
  cream

Buttercream

30 g/2 tablespoons salted butter,
  softened
160 g/1⅓ cup fondant icing/
  confectioners' sugar, sifted

*a large baking sheet lined
  with baking parchment
  or a silicon mat*

*3 piping bags, 2 with round
  nozzles/tips and 1 with a small
  star nozzle/tip*

Makes 12

Preheat the oven to 200°C (400°F) Gas 6.

Spoon the choux pastry/paste into a piping bag fitted with a round nozzle/tip and pipe 12 rings about 5 cm/2 inches in diameter and 12 small balls onto the baking sheets, a small distance apart. Pat down any peaks in the pastry/paste using a clean wet finger. Sprinkle a little water into the bottom of the oven to create steam which will help the *religieuse* to rise.

Bake in the oven for 10 minutes, then reduce the oven temperature to 180°C (350°F) Gas 4 and bake for a further 15–20 minutes until the pastry is crisp. Remove from the oven and using a sharp knife cut a small slit into each of the rings and balls to allow any steam to escape. Leave to cool then make a small hole in the bottom of each ring and ball, ready for piping the filling in later.

For the icing, mix together the icing/confectioners' sugar with the espresso coffee until you have a smooth, thick icing. Add the coffee gradually as you may not need it all. Spread the icing over the tops of the rings and the balls. Place a chocolate coffee bean or chocolate decoration on top of the balls and leave for the icing to set.

For the filling, pour half of the cooled coffee into a mixing bowl with the cream and whisk to stiff peaks. Spoon into a piping bag with a round nozzle/tip and carefully pipe cream into each ring and ball, taking care not to touch the icing. Pipe a small mound of cream into the centre of each ring and place one of the balls on top.

For the buttercream, whisk together the remaining coffee, butter and icing/confectioners' sugar, and whisk until light and creamy so that the buttercream holds peaks when you pick up the whisk. Place into the piping bag fitted with the small star nozzle/tip and pipe pretty lines of decoration onto the *religieuse* as shown in the photograph. Serve straight away.

PARIS BREST

This delicacy of choux pastry rings filled with praline cream was created in 1891 to celebrate the Paris to Brest cycle ride. Its classic shape was said to represent the wheels of the bicycles.

1 quantity Basic Choux
  Pastry/Paste (see page 7)
20 g hazelnuts, roasted, skinned
  and chopped

Praline
100 g/½ cup caster/granulated
  sugar
80 g/¾ cup hazelnuts, roasted,
  skinned and chopped

Filling
300 ml/1¼ cups double/heavy
  cream
1 tablespoon hazelnut butter
icing/confectioners' sugar, for
  dusting

*2 large baking sheets lined
  with baking parchment
  or a silicon mat*

*2 piping bags, 1 with a round
  nozzle/tip and 1 with a large
  star nozzle/tip*

Makes 9

Preheat the oven to 200°C (400°F) Gas 6. Spoon the choux pastry/paste into one of the piping bags and pipe 9 rings about 7 cm/3 inches in diameter onto the baking sheets, a small distance apart. Pat down any peaks in the pastry/paste using a clean wet finger. Sprinkle the pastry/paste with the hazelnuts. Sprinkle a little water into the bottom of the oven to create steam which will help the choux pastry/paste to rise. Bake in the oven for 10 minutes, then reduce the oven temperature to 180°C (350°F) Gas 4 and bake for a further 15–20 minutes until the pastry is crisp. Remove from the oven and cut a slit into each ring to allow any steam to escape. Leave to cool.

For the praline, heat the sugar in a saucepan until melted and golden brown. Do not stir the pan as the sugar is cooking but swirl it to ensure that the sugar does not burn. Spread the hazelnuts out on a greased baking sheet or silicon mat and carefully pour over the melted sugar. Leave to cool and then blitz in a blender to very fine crumbs.

For the filling, whisk together the cream and hazelnut butter in a mixing bowl to stiff peaks. Stir in the praline with a spatula, reserving a little powder to sprinkle over the top of the rings.

Spoon the cream into the second piping bag fitted with the star nozzle/tip. Carefully, cut each ring in half horizontally with a sharp knife. Pipe a swirl of cream into the bottom of each bun. Top each with the hazelnut covered rings and then dust with icing/confectioners' sugar, sprinkle with a little of the praline powder and serve immediately. These are best eaten on the day they are made.

STRUDEL CREAM PUFFS

These light cream puffs are inspired by the popular dessert apple strudel.

2 quantities Basic Choux
Pastry/Paste (see page 7)

Baked apples

4 large cooking apples
120 g/4½ cups sultanas/golden
raisins
1 teaspoon ground cinnamon
3 tablespoon golden syrup
60 ml/⅓ cup water

Caramel glaze

50 g/1½ cups caster/granulated
sugar
1 tablespoon unsalted butter
a pinch of salt
60 ml/¼ cup double/heavy cream
180 g/1½ cups fondant icing/
confectioners' sugar, sifted

To assemble

400 ml/1½ cups double/heavy
cream, whipped to stiff peaks

an apple corer

*2 baking sheets lined with
baking parchment*

*2 piping bags, 1 with a large
round nozzle/tip and 1 with
a large star nozzle/tip*

Makes 26

Preheat the oven to 180°C (350°F) Gas 4. Begin by preparing the apples. Core the apples and using a sharp knife cut a slit horizontally around the apples. Place the apples in a roasting pan. Mix the sultanas/golden raisins with the cinnamon and fill the core of each apple with them. Spoon some golden syrup over the filled core of each apple and add the water to the pan. Bake the apples for 40 minutes then turn the temperature down to 150°C (300°F) Gas 2 and cook for a further 30 minutes. Remove from the oven and leave to cool. Discard the skins and mix the apple, sultanas and syrup together.

Preheat the oven to 200°C (400°F) Gas 6. Spoon the choux pastry/paste into the piping bag with a round nozzle/tip and pipe 26 balls of pastry/paste onto the baking sheets, a small distance apart. Pat down any peaks in the pastry using a clean wet finger. Sprinkle a little water into the bottom of the oven to create steam. Bake each sheet in the oven for 10 minutes, then reduce the oven temperature to 180°C (350°F) Gas 4 and bake for a further 15–20 minutes until the pastry is crisp. Remove from the oven and cut a small slit into each cream puff to allow the steam to escape. Leave to cool.

For the caramel glaze, place the sugar, butter and salt in a saucepan and simmer over a gentle heat until the sugar and butter have melted and the caramel is golden brown. Remove from the heat and allow to cool for a few minutes then pour in the cream and whisk together until the caramel is smooth and glossy. Strain to remove any crystallized sugar and leave to cool. Mix the icing/confectioners' sugar into the caramel sauce, adding water if necessary, then dip each bun into the glaze and leave on a rack to set.

To serve, cut each cream puff in half. Spoon the cream into the piping bag with a star nozzle/tip and pipe a swirl of cream into the bottom of each puff. Top with a spoonful of the cooled apple. Top with the caramel glazed cream puffs and serve straight away.

PLUM & ALMOND PUFFS

Here plums and almonds sit atop thin layers of puff pastry and are brushed with a sticky, sweet honey glaze.

400 g/14 oz. ready-made/ready-rolled puff pastry

plenty of plain/all-purpose flour, for dusting

6–8 ripe red plums, pitted and thinly sliced

2 tablespoons caster/superfine sugar

2 tablespoons flaked/slivered almonds

Honey glaze

50 g/3 tablespoons unsalted butter

50 g/¼ cup vanilla sugar

1 tablespoon honey

1 teaspoon ground cinnamon

icing/confectioners' sugar, for dusting

2 large baking sheets, greased and lined with baking parchment

Serves 2–4

Preheat the oven to 180°C (350°F) Gas 4.

Dust a clean work surface with flour and roll out the pastry into a rectangle about 40 x 20 cm/16 x 8 inches and to a thickness of about 3–5 mm/⅛ x ¼ inch. Trim the edges using a sharp knife. It is important to use a downward cutting motion with the knife rather than dragging it through the pastry as this may compress the pastry leaves, resulting in less rising of the pastry. Cut the rectangle in two and transfer to the baking sheets. (You can make one large slice if you prefer but the pastry is quite fragile and is easier to transfer in two smaller slices.) Using a sharp knife, score a thin line around each pastry slice, about 1 cm/½ inch from the edge.

Cover the inner square with thin slices of plum and sprinkle with the caster/superfine sugar and almonds. Make sure that you do not cover the scored line as this will prevent the pastry from rising. Bake in the preheated oven for 20–25 minutes, until the pastry is golden brown and has risen.

Meanwhile make the honey glaze. Put the butter, sugar, honey and cinnamon in a small saucepan with 1 tablespoon water. Heat until the sugar has dissolved and the mixture is smooth and syrupy. When the slices are cooked, remove them from the oven and brush each with the toffee glaze. Serve warm with whipped cream.

These puffs are best eaten on the day they are made.

PEAR, MASCARPONE & ORANGE TARTLETS

Using ready-made and ready-rolled puff pastry makes life easy here. Slices of plum or apple would also work well as a topping for these tangy pastries.

300-g/10-oz package chilled
  ready-made/ready-rolled puff
  pastry
40 g/4 tablespoons unsalted
  butter
125 g/½ cup mascarpone
3 tablespoons caster/
  granulated sugar, plus extra
  for sprinkling
finely grated zest of
  1 small unwaxed orange
75 g/½ cup ground almonds
1 large egg yolk
4 ripe but firm small pears,
  cored and thinly sliced
3–4 tablespoons smooth apricot
  jam/jelly
4 tablespoons toasted
  flaked/slivered almonds

*2–3 large baking sheets,
  lined with baking parchment
  and greased*

Makes 12

Preheat the oven to 220°C (425°F) Gas 7. Take the pastry out of the fridge. Melt the butter in a small pan and leave to cool slightly.

Put the mascarpone, sugar, orange zest, ground almonds and egg yolk in a bowl and mix. Refrigerate until needed.

Halve the pastry and roll one half out on a lightly floured work surface until it is about 2 mm/⅛ inch – any thicker than that and the pastry won't crisp up in the oven. Trim the edges with a sharp knife to make a 21 x 24-cm/8 x 20-inch piece, then cut that into six 7 x 12-cm/3 x 5-inch rectangles. Arrange the rectangles on one of the prepared baking sheets.

Repeat with the other half of the pastry.

Brush the edges of each rectangle with the melted butter and sprinkle a little sugar over them. Put 2 teaspoons of the mascarpone mixture in the centre of each rectangle. Spread the mixture out using a small knife, leaving a border of about 1 cm/½ inch all the way round.

Top each tart with overlapping slices of pear and scatter a little more sugar over the top. Bake the tarts in the preheated oven for 15 minutes, or until the pastry is golden and crisp. Transfer to a wire rack.

Warm the apricot jam/jelly in a small pan, then use to brush over the pear slices. Sprinkle the flaked almonds over the top, then leave to cool before serving.

INDIVIDUAL APPLE TARTS

Little individual apple tarts are so quick and easy to make with ready-rolled puff pastry. You could also try making this tart with a layer of ready-made caramel (look for jars of dulce de leche) under the apple, another delightful coffeetime treat.

375 g/12 oz. ready-rolled puff
   pastry
4–5 apples
4–5 tablespoons honey

a 6-cm/2½-inch round pastry
   cutter

1–2 baking sheets, greased and
   lined with baking parchment

Makes 6

Preheat the oven to 200°C (400°F) Gas 6.

Roll out the pastry on a lightly floured work surface. Cut out 6 circles about 6 cm/2½ inches in diameter and prick the bases lightly with a fork. Lay them on the prepared baking sheets.

Peel and core the apples and cut them into very thin slices; arrange them neatly over the pastry so they overlap. Bake for 6–8 minutes, until golden.

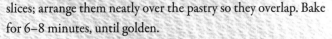

Warm the honey in a small saucepan over a gentle heat and brush carefully over the apples. Serve the tarts warm or cold.

CHOCOLATE AND ALMOND TARTLETS

These delicious chocolate and almond cakes are a speciality of the Abruzzo region. More often than not they have a pastry lid too but they can be a little heavy on the pastry that way, so this recipe is an open tartlet version. They are always very well received.

Pastry
175 g/1½ sticks butter, softened
75 g/⅓ cup caster/granulated
　sugar
1 egg yolk
250 g/2 cups plain/all-purpose
　flour

Chocolate and almond filling
100 g/3½ oz. dark/bittersweet
　chocolate
50 g/⅓ cup ground almonds
50 g/¼ cup caster/granulated
　sugar
1 egg white
icing/confectioners' sugar, for
　dusting

*a 6-cm/2½-inch round pastry
　cutter*

*a 12-cup tartlet or bun pan,
　greased*

Makes 12

Preheat the oven to 180°C (350°F) Gas 4.

First make the pastry. Beat the butter and sugar together until smooth. Add the egg yolk and beat again until the egg has been fully incorporated. Stir in the flour and gather the mixture together to form a smooth but not sticky dough. Divide the dough in half and freeze one portion to use later.

Roll out the dough on a lightly floured work surface until it is about 2 mm thick, then stamp out 12 circles and press one gently into each cup in the greased tartlet pan.

Meanwhile, chop the chocolate into small nuggets and put them in a large mixing bowl. Add the ground almonds and sugar. Stir in the egg white.

Fill the tartlet cases with a spoonful of the mixture and transfer to the oven. Bake for 6–8 minutes, until the filling has set and the pastry is golden. Remove from the oven and leave to cool in the pan. Dust with icing/confectioners' sugar and serve.

PECAN AND BOURBON TARTLETS

These smart, nutty, irresistible little tarts are perfect for winter entertaining.

250 g/2 cups plain/all-purpose
flour
125 g/1 stick unsalted butter,
chilled and cubed
85 g/5 tablespoons golden
caster/granulated sugar
1 egg

Date sponge
60 g/2 oz. Medjool dates, pitted
30 ml/2 tablespoons
double/heavy cream
30 g/2 tablespoons unsalted
butter, melted
30 g/2½ tablespoons light
brown soft/packed sugar
1 egg
a few drops of vanilla extract
55 g/½ cup plain/all-purpose flour
1 teaspoon baking powder

Pecan bourbon filling
1 tablespoon Bourbon whiskey
40 g/3 tablespoons light brown
soft/packed sugar
55 ml/¼ cup golden syrup
1 egg, beaten
20 g/1½ tablespoons unsalted
butter, melted
60 g/½ cup shelled pecan nuts,
roughly chopped plus 18
pecan halves, to decorate

*6 x 9-cm/3½-inch loose-based
fluted tartlet pans, greased*

Makes 6

Preheat the oven to 180°C (350°F) Gas 4.

Put the flour, butter and sugar in a mixer and blitz until you get crumbs. Add the egg and mix again. Take the dough out of the mixer and bring together into a ball. If you prefer, you can make the dough by hand, but it's easier to do this if the butter is grated or very finely chopped.

Put the dough on a lightly floured surface and roll with a rolling pin until 3–4 mm/⅛ inch thick. Line the tartlet pans with the pastry and trim the excess dough neatly around the edges. Refrigerate while you make the filling.

To make the date sponge, blitz the dates to a paste in a food processor or simply chop them very finely. Mix with the cream and 1 tablespoon water and set aside.

Put the butter and sugar in a mixing bowl and mix well, then add the egg, vanilla, flour and baking powder. Finally, add date mixture and fold in well.

Remove the tartlet shells from the fridge and spoon about 1½ tablespoons of the date sponge into them. Bake in the preheated oven for 15 minutes, then remove from the oven (leaving the oven on).

In the meantime, make the pecan bourbon filling. Put the Bourbon, sugar and syrup in a mixing bowl and mix well. Add the egg, mix well, then stir in the melted butter and pecan nuts.

Spoon the pecan bourbon filling on top of the tartlets and spread evenly. Decorate with 3 pecan halves and return to the oven for another 10 minutes. Remove from the oven and leave to cool before serving.

PRALINE APPLE STRUDEL

Praline powder is a cinch to prepare and makes a great addition to many desserts – apple or otherwise. Here it teams up with the crispy flaky pastry to lift what would be an ordinary strudel well above the average.

450 g/1 lb. tart eating apples, such as Cox's, Orange Pippin or Braeburn, peeled, cored and chopped

75 g/¼ cup dried fruit, such as sultanas/golden raisins, cranberries or sour cherries

100 g/½ cup light brown/packed sugar

1 teaspoon ground cinnamon

1 tablespoon unsalted butter

6 sheets filo/phyllo pastry (thawed if frozen)

50 g/4 tablespoons unsalted butter, melted

icing/confectioners' sugar, to dust

whipped cream, crème fraîche or sour cream, to serve

Praline

75 g/½ cup shelled pecans

40 g/¼ cup caster/granulated sugar

a baking sheet, greased and lined with baking parchment

Serves 6–8

To make the praline, combine the pecans and sugar in a non-stick heavy-based frying pan/skillet and cook over medium/high heat, stirring constantly, until the sugar hardens and coats the nuts. Transfer to a plate to cool, then process in a coffee grinder or small food processor until ground to a coarse powder. Set aside.

In a large saucepan, combine the apples, dried fruit, brown sugar, cinnamon and 1 tablespoon butter. Cook over medium heat until the apples are soft and the juices have evaporated, about 15 minutes. Remove from the heat and let cool.

Preheat the oven to 190°C (375°F) Gas 5.

Put 2 sheets of filo/phyllo on the prepared baking sheet and brush with some melted butter. Sprinkle with a little praline.

Top with 2 more sheets of filo/phyllo and repeat. Top with 2 more sheets of filo/phyllo. Spread the apple mixture in an even layer over the top sheet of filo/phyllo. Sprinkle with more praline mixture, then carefully roll up from a long end, like a Swiss/jelly roll. Use the paper to help you roll, if necessary.

The seam side needs to be on the bottom. Brush with a little more melted butter, sprinkle with any remaining praline and bake in the preheated oven until crisp and golden, about 25–35 minutes.

Remove from the oven and let cool slightly. Dust with a little icing/confectioners' sugar, slice and serve warm with whipped cream, crème fraîche or sour cream.

CHOCOLATE AND PEAR TART

This chocolate and pear tart is rich and fabulous and makes a wonderful treat with a good espresso. It also makes a fantastic dessert served with a generous helping of vanilla ice cream on top.

Pastry

175 g/1½ sticks unsalted butter, softened

50 g/¼ cup caster/granulated sugar

1 egg yolk

250 g/2 cups plain/all-purpose flour

Chocolate and pear filling

200 g/1 stick plus 6 tablespoons butter

200 g/1 cup caster/granulated sugar

3 eggs, beaten

200 g/1⅓ cups ground almonds

2 tablespoons plain/all-purpose flour

100 g/3½ oz. dark/bittersweet chocolate, melted

4 ripe but firm pears

caster/superfine sugar, for dusting

a 23-cm/9-inch tart pan with removable base

Serves 6–8

Preheat the oven to 180°C (350°F) Gas 4.

First make the pastry. Beat the butter and sugar together until smooth. Add the egg yolk and beat again until thoroughly mixed. Stir in the flour and work the mixture lightly until it forms a smooth but not sticky dough. Divide the dough in half and freeze one portion to use later.

Roll out the dough on a lightly floured work surface and use to line the tart pan. Chill for 30 minutes or so if time allows.

To make the filling, beat the butter and sugar together until light and fluffy. Add the eggs, ground almonds and flour and beat until smooth. Stir in the chocolate. Spoon into the pastry case and smooth gently using a palette knife.

Peel the pears, cut them in half lengthways and remove the cores. Cut them horizontally into 5 mm/¼ inch slices and lay them evenly on the filling. Start in the centre and fan them towards the crust to open out the slices a little. Bake the tart for about 45 minutes, or until the almond mixture is firm and the pastry is golden. Leave to cool, dust with caster/superfine sugar and serve.

COFFEE AND CHOCOLATE TART

Take care not to overcook the filling; you're aiming for a sort of fudgy, chocolate brownie texture. Kahlúa adds a distinctive, boozy, coffee kick to this tart, but you could substitute Tia Maria for a slightly sweeter result with hints of chocolate, or use any creamy liqueur. Reduce the quantity if using hard spirits such as brandy or rum.

Pastry

175 g/1½ sticks unsalted butter, softened
50 g/¼ cup caster/granulated sugar
1 egg yolk
270 g/2 cups plus 1 tablespoon plain/all-purpose flour, sifted

Coffee filling

125 g/1 stick unsalted butter
250 g/1¼ cups muscovado sugar
10 g/2 tablespoons espresso beans, finely ground
90 ml/6 tablespoons Kahlúa liqueur
2 eggs, lightly beaten
50 g/⅓ cup self-raising/rising flour, sifted

To decorate

40 g/1½ oz. dark/bittersweet chocolate, broken into pieces
1 handful whole coffee beans

a 20-cm/8-inch tart pan with removable base

Serves 6–8

First make the pastry. Cream the butter and sugar together until light and fluffy. Add the egg yolk and stir until fully incorporated and smooth. Slowly add the flour and mix until the pastry forms a ball, taking care not to overwork the dough.

Divide the dough in half and freeze one portion for another time. Wrap the remaining pastry in clingfilm/plastic wrap and leave to rest for 20 minutes. Roll out the pastry on a lightly floured work surface and use to line the tart pan. Refrigerate until needed.

Preheat the oven to 180°C (350°F) Gas 4 while you make the filling. Heat the butter and sugar together in a saucepan until melted. Add the espresso grounds and Kahlúa, stir in the eggs and then fold in the flour lightly but thoroughly. Pour the mixture into the chilled pastry case and cook for 20–25 minutes, checking after 20 minutes. Remove from the oven and cool.

Melt the chocolate in a small bowl set over a saucepan of gently simmering water (or microwave on full power for 1–2 minutes, stirring halfway through). Dip the whole coffee beans into the melted chocolate. Arrange the chocolate beans in clusters around the edge of the tart and serve.

PECAN & CHOCOLATE TART WITH MAPLE SYRUP

Genuine maple syrup has a unique kind of sweetness that adds something extra to this rather decadent dish. Best saved for a special occasion, it's very rich and a little goes a long way.

Pâte sucrée

320 g/2 sticks plus 6 tablespoons salted butter, chilled and cubed

160 g/¾ cup caster/granulated sugar

500 g/4 cups plain/all-purpose flour

1 egg

Filling

200 g/¾ cup maple syrup

20 g/1½ cups muscovado sugar

20 g/1½ tablespoons salted butter

80 g/2½ oz. dark/bittersweet chocolate, finely chopped

3 eggs

150 g/1 cup pecan halves

a 23-cm/9-inch tart pan with removable base

baking beans

Serves 10–12

Put the butter, sugar and flour in a large bowl and rub between your fingertips until the texture resembles fine breadcrumbs. (You can add orange or lemon zest at this point if desired.) Add the egg and work the mixture with your hands to a smooth paste. Wrap the dough in clingfilm/plastic wrap and refrigerate for about 30 minutes until firm.

Preheat the oven to 190°C (375°F) Gas 5.

Roll out the chilled pastry, line the tart pan and blind bake following the method on page 69. Remove from the oven and reduce the oven temperature to 150°C (300°F) Gas 2.

To make the filling, put the maple syrup, sugar and butter into a saucepan and stir over medium heat until melted. Remove from the heat and add the chocolate, stirring until it has melted and the mixture is smooth. Add the eggs and beat into the mixture. Finally, stir in the pecans.

Pour the mixture into the tart case and bake in the preheated oven for 30–35 minutes or until the filling is just set.

The tart can be served warm or at room temperature. It will keep for 2–3 days in an airtight container.

CHERRY AND ALMOND TART

In May and June the south of Italy is bursting at the seams with cherries, so you'll very likely see a cherry tart or two if you visit then. This cherry tart is a stunner, with crisp pastry encasing a gorgeous frangipane filling, speckled with fresh cherries. See if you can resist a second slice.

Pastry

175 g/1½ sticks unsalted butter, softened

50 g/¼ cup caster/granulated sugar

1 egg yolk

250 g/2 cups plain/all-purpose flour

Filling

200 g/1 stick plus 6 tablespoons unsalted butter, softened

200 g/1 cup caster/granulated sugar

3 eggs, beaten

200 g/1⅓ cups ground almonds

2 tablespoons plain/all-purpose flour

250 g/9 oz. fresh cherries, pitted

icing/confectioners' sugar, for dusting

a 23-cm/9-inch tart pan with removable base

Makes 6–8

First make the pastry. Beat the butter and sugar together until smooth. Add the egg yolk and beat again until thoroughly mixed. Stir in the flour and work the mixture lightly until it forms a smooth but not sticky dough. Divide the dough in half and freeze one portion to use another time.

Roll out the dough on a lightly floured work surface and use to line the tart pan. Chill for 30 minutes if time allows.

Preheat the oven to 180°C (350°F) Gas 4 while you make the filling.

Beat the butter and sugar together until light and fluffy. Add the eggs, ground almonds and flour and beat until smooth. Spoon into the prepared pastry case and smooth gently using a palette knife.

Gently push the cherries a little way into the almond mixture, distributing them evenly. Bake the tart for about 45 minutes, or until the almond mixture is golden and set.

Leave to cool and dust with icing sugar before serving.

FIG & MARSALA CROSTATA

Marsala combines perfectly with dried figs to make a superbly flavoured filling.

Filling

550 g/19 oz. dried figs, roughly chopped

440 ml/1¾ cups Marsala

40 g/3 tablespoons dark brown sugar

2 cinnamon sticks

a pinch of ground cloves

Pâte sucrée

1 teaspoon fennel seeds

320 g/2 sticks plus 5 tablespoons salted butter, chilled and cubed

160 g/¾ cup caster/granulated sugar

500 g/4 cups plain/all-purpose flour

orange or lemon zest (optional)

1 egg

23-cm/9-inch tart pan with removable base

Serves 8–10

To make the filling, put the ingredients and 300 ml/1¾ cups water in a large saucepan set over medium heat and bring to the boil. Turn down the heat and simmer for 40 minutes or until the liquid has reduced by at least half. Remove from the heat and allow to cool slightly. Remove the cinnamon sticks, then pour the mixture into a food processor and blend for no more than 10 seconds – you want a sticky paste. Refrigerate until chilled and thickened.

To make the pastry, bruise the fennel seeds with a pestle and mortar. Put the butter, sugar and flour in a large bowl and rub between your fingertips until the texture resembles fine breadcrumbs. Stir the bruised fennel seeds into the bowl (add orange or lemon zest at this point if desired). Add the egg and work the mixture with your hands to a smooth paste.

Divide the pastry in half, wrap in clingfilm/plastic wrap and refrigerate for 15 minutes. You won't need all of it, so freeze one half for another time.

Preheat the oven to 170°C (325°F) Gas 3.

Roll out the chilled pastry on a lightly floured surface to form a circle about 30 cm/12 inches in diameter and about 3 mm/⅛ inch thick. Drape the pastry over the rolling pin and carefully transfer it to the tart pan. Gently mould the pastry into the base and sides. The pastry is fragile to handle but any gaps can be repaired using surplus pastry. Trim the top edge with a sharp knife. Reserve any surplus pastry for decoration.

Spoon the chilled filling into the tart case and spread level with a palette knife. Roll out the reserved pastry and cut into 1-cm/½-inch wide strips. Weave the pastry strips in a lattice pattern across the surface of the filling. Place the tart on a baking sheet and bake in the preheated oven for 45–55 minutes or until golden brown. Remove from the oven and let cool slightly in the pan.

GERMAN CHOCOLATE CHEESECAKE

Dulce de leche, coconut and pecans pair beautifully with tangy cheesecake.

600 g/1 lb. 5 oz. HobNobs or
graham crackers
75–100 g/¾–1 stick unsalted
butter, melted

Fudge icing

250 ml/1 cup whipping cream
65 g/3 tablespoons golden syrup
350 g/12 oz. dark/bittersweet
chocolate, chopped
1 teaspoon vanilla extract
75 g/5 tablespoons unsalted
butter, cut into cubes, chilled

Filling

800 g/1 lb. 12 oz. cream cheese
225 g/1 cup plus 1 tablespoon
caster/superfine sugar
2 eggs
50 g/½ cup plus 1 tablespoon
cornflour/starch
250 ml/1 cup whipping cream
1 teaspoon vanilla extract

Topping

100 g/4 oz. dulce de leche
5 tablespoons soft shredded
coconut, lightly toasted
75 g/⅔ cup pecan halves, lightly
toasted and crushed

melted dark/bittersweet chocolate,
for drizzling

*25-cm/10-inch cake pan, greased
and lined with baking parchment*

Serves 10–12

To make the crust, crush the biscuits/cookies until you get fine crumbs. Add the melted butter – the amount of butter you will need is variable (see page 149). Press the mixture into the prepared cake pan and pat until level.

To make the fudge icing, put the cream and golden syrup in a medium saucepan and bring to a boil. Put the chocolate in a large, heatproof bowl. As soon as the cream mixture has come to a boil, pour it over the chocolate. Set aside for 1 minute. Using a small balloon whisk placed in the middle of the bowl, stir with very small motions. It will look like nothing is happening until eventually a very shiny, thick, glossy mixture forms. Gradually stir in wider motions to incorporate more cream into the emulsion until it's fully combined. Add the vanilla extract and butter and mix until well combined. Set aside to let the chocolate stiffen before using.

Preheat the oven to 125°C (240°F) Gas 1.

Put the cream cheese and sugar in a bowl and beat until well mixed and the sugar has dissolved. Slowly incorporate the eggs, one at a time, beating until thoroughly combined before adding the next. Sift the cornflour/starch into the mixture and stir until combined. Add the cream and vanilla extract and mix until combined. Pour the mixture into the cake pan over the crust and bake in the preheated oven for 1 hour until the middle is slightly jiggly and the top doesn't look shiny or wet any more.

Remove from the oven and let cool in the pan for 1 hour. Refrigerate overnight.

Unmould the cheesecake by turning it upside down on a plate or board, then turning upright again. Spread a layer of fudge icing over the cheesecake. Warm the dulce de leche in a microwave for 20 seconds, and drizzle over the fudge icing. Sprinkle the coconut, pecans and some melted chocolate all over.

CHOCOLATE PEANUT BUTTER CHEESECAKE

This recipe uses honey-roasted peanuts for the top but, if you want to be adventurous, salty, spiced peanuts would add an interesting twist.

400 g/14 oz. finely crushed Chocolate Peanut Butter Biscotti (see page 36)

75–100 g/¾–1 stick unsalted butter, melted

Filling

800 g/1 lb. 12 oz. cream cheese

225 g/1 cup plus 1 tablespoon caster/superfine sugar

2 eggs

50 g/½ cup plus 1 tablespoon cornflour/starch

250 ml/1 cup whipping cream

1 teaspoon vanilla extract

200 g/7 oz. dark/semi-sweet chocolate, melted

Topping

Fudge Icing (see German Chocolate Cheesecake page 146)

as much peanut butter as you like (chunky or smooth)

chocolate curls, to decorate

honey-roasted peanuts, to decorate

a baking sheet, lined with baking parchment

a 25-cm/10-inch cake pan, greased and lined with baking parchment

Serves 10–12

Preheat the oven to 125°C (240°F) Gas ½.

To make the crust, crush the Chocolate Peanut Butter Biscotti until you get fine crumbs. Add the melted butter – the amount of butter you will need is variable. Test by grabbing a bit of the mixture and squeezing into your hand to make a ball, then releasing your hand. The mixture should hold its shape, but also fall apart when touched slightly. If it doesn't hold its shape, add more butter. If it holds its shape too well, add more biscotti to absorb the butter, otherwise your crust will be too hard. Press the mixture into the prepared cake pan and pat down until level.

Put the cream cheese and sugar in a bowl and beat until well mixed and the sugar has dissolved. Slowly incorporate the eggs, one at a time, beating until thoroughly combined before adding the next. Sift the cornflour/starch into the mixture and stir until thoroughly combined. Add the cream and vanilla extract and mix until combined. Transfer half the mixture to a separate bowl and fold in the melted chocolate.

Pour both mixtures into the cake pan over the crust and swirl with a fork to create a marbled effect. Bake in the preheated oven for 1 hour until the middle is slightly jiggly and the top doesn't look shiny or wet any more.

Remove from the oven and let cool in the pan for 1 hour. Refrigerate overnight.

Unmould the cheesecake by turning it upside down on a plate or board, then turning it upright again.

Spread a layer of Fudge Icing over the cheesecake. Warm the peanut butter slightly and spoon over the fudge icing in nice big dollops. Swirl with fork to create a marbled effect. Decorate with chocolate curls and honey-roasted peanuts.

CAPPUCCINO CHEESECAKE

Built on a mouth-watering cookie base with a hint of dark, bitter chocolate, this smooth, creamy mascarpone cheesecake is topped with a layer of glossy white sour cream and dusted with cocoa, so that a slice really does resemble a cup of cappuccino.

150 g/5 oz. dark chocolate-covered digestive biscuits/graham crackers

60 g/4 tablespoons unsalted butter, melted

500 g/1 lb. 4 oz. mascarpone

125 ml/⅔ cup crème fraîche or double/heavy cream

3 tablespoons instant coffee granules, dissolved in 3 tablespoons just-boiled water

125 g/⅔ cup caster/granulated sugar, plus 1½ tablespoons for the topping

4 eggs, beaten

240 ml/1 cup sour cream

cocoa powder, to dust

a 20-cm/9-inch springform cake pan, greased

Serves 8

Put the digestive biscuits/graham crackers in a food processor and process until they become crumbs, then combine with the melted butter. Tip the mixture into the prepared cake pan and smooth out to make an even base. Cover and chill for 30 minutes.

Preheat the oven to 180°C (350°F) Gas 4.

Beat together the mascarpone and crème fraîche or double/heavy cream until smooth, then stir in the coffee and sugar. Stir in the eggs until well mixed.

Wrap the base and sides of the pan in two single sheets of aluminium foil, then pour the mascarpone mixture over the crumb crust. Put in a roasting pan and pour water around the cake pan so that it reaches half to two-thirds of the way up the sides. Bake for about 50 minutes until set but still soft.

Meanwhile, stir the remaining 1½ tablespoons sugar into the sour cream. Remove the cheesecake from the oven, gently spoon over the sour cream, spreading it out evenly, then return to the oven for 10 minutes.

Remove from the oven and leave to cool, then cover and chill for at least 4 hours or overnight. To serve, carefully unmould and dust with cocoa powder.

Chapter 5

MUFFINS & CAKES

CHOCOLATE HEAVEN MUFFINS

These muffins are bursting with chocolate and are as easy as pie to rustle up. For the ultimate chocolate experience, eat them fresh from the oven.

75 g/5 tablespoons unsalted butter

75 g/2½ oz. dark/bittersweet chocolate (about 50% cocoa solids)

75 g/2½ oz. milk/semisweet chocolate

50 g/2 oz. white chocolate

100 g/½ cup sour cream

3 tablespoons milk

50 g/¼ cup light muscovado or packed light brown soft sugar

2 eggs

175 g/1⅓ cups plain/all-purpose flour

2 tablespoons cocoa powder

1 tablespoon baking powder

a pinch of salt

1 tablespoon demerara sugar

a 6-hole muffin pan, lined with muffin cases

Makes 6

Preheat the oven to 200°C (400°F) Gas 6.

Melt the butter in a small pan and let cool slightly.

Chop the three types of chocolate into small chunks.

In a large mixing bowl and using a balloon whisk, whisk together the sour cream, milk, muscovado sugar, eggs and melted butter.

Sift in the flour, cocoa and baking powder. Sprinkle in the salt and add all the chopped chocolate. Using a large metal spoon, fold everything together until combined, but don't over-mix.

Divide the mixture between the muffin cases. Sprinkle each muffin with a little demerara sugar. Bake the muffins in the preheated oven for 20 minutes – by which time they will be risen, but still very slightly unset in the middle. They will continue to cook as they cool.

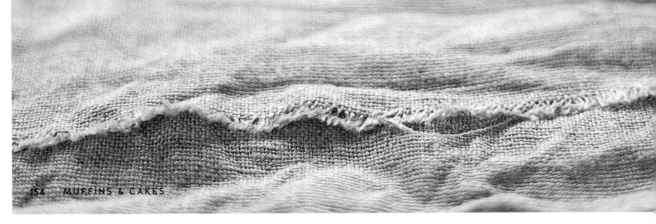

ALMOND CHERRY MUFFINS

These muffins are kind of a play on the friand and the wonderful muffin. The yogurt and ground almonds add a bit of lightness to the crumb and the tart cherries will wake you up in the morning.

240 g/1¼ cups caster/superfine sugar

grated zest of 1 unwaxed lemon

150 g/1 cup plain/all-purpose flour, plus 1 tablespoon for coating the cherries

70 g/½ cup ground almonds

2 teaspoons baking powder

a pinch of salt

3 eggs

130 g/½ cup Greek yogurt

½ teaspoon vanilla extract

¼ teaspoon almond extract

80 ml/⅓ cup sunflower oil

50 g/3½ tablespoons unsalted butter, melted

120 g/1¼ cups pitted sour cherries

about 50 g/⅔ cup flaked/slivered almonds, or sprinkling

a 12-hole muffin pan, lined with muffin cases

Makes 12

Preheat the oven to 170°C (340°F) Gas 5.

Whiz the sugar and lemon zest in an electric mixer with paddle attachment (or rub with your bare hands) until the sugar smells super lemony. Add the flour, ground almonds, baking powder and salt and mix well.

In a separate bowl, combine the eggs, yogurt and vanilla and almond extracts. Pour into the flour mixture and stir until just combined and no traces of flour remain. Fold in the oil and melted butter.

In another bowl, toss the cherries in the extra flour until thoroughly coated, then fold into the muffin batter.

Spoon the mixture into the prepared muffin cases and scatter the almonds over the tops. Bake in the preheated oven for 20–25 minutes. A wooden skewer inserted in the middle should come out clean, and the tops of the muffins should feel springy to the touch. Remove the muffins from the muffin pan and eat immediately.

APPLE SPICE MUFFINS

A virtuous mix of apples, raisins, wholemeal flour, buttermilk and loads of warm spices, these muffins are perfect for breakfast, brunch or lunch boxes. If you have fussy children who don't like 'bits', the apple can be coarsely grated and the raisins omitted.

140 g/1 cup plain/all-purpose flour

85 g/⅓ cup wholemeal/wheat flour

145 g/1 cup dark brown sugar

1 teaspoon bicarbonate of/baking soda

¼ teaspoon baking powder

1 teaspoon ground cinnamon

½ teaspoon each ground nutmeg, ginger and cloves

a pinch of sea salt

250 ml/1 cup buttermilk

125 ml/½ cup vegetable oil

1 teaspoon vanilla extract

1 tart apple, peeled, cored and finely chopped

50 g/2 oz. raisins

Frosting

400 g/2 x 8-oz. packs cream cheese (not low-fat)

115 g/1 stick unsalted butter, softened

120 g/1 cup icing/confectioners' sugar

1 teaspoon vanilla extract

a 12-hole muffin pan, lined with muffin cases

Makes 12

For the frosting, put the cream cheese, butter, sugar and vanilla in a bowl and beat with a hand-held electric whisk until smooth. Refrigerate until needed.

Preheat the oven to 180°C (350°F) Gas 4. In a mixing bowl, combine the plain/all-purpose flour, wholemeal/wheat flour, sugar, bicarbonate of/baking soda, baking powder, cinnamon, nutmeg, ginger, cloves and salt. Mix well to combine.

In a separate bowl, combine the buttermilk, oil and vanilla extract. Stir, then add this mixture to the dry ingredients, folding in with a spatula to blend thoroughly. Add the apple and raisins and mix just to combine.

Drop spoonfuls of the mixture into the paper cases, filling each almost to the top. Bake in the preheated oven until puffed and a skewer inserted in the centre of a muffin comes out clean, about 25–35 minutes.

Transfer to a wire rack, let cool completely then spread the top of each muffin with frosting before serving.

BLUEBERRY STREUSEL MUFFINS

Muffins should be eaten the moment baked – the difference between a freshly baked muffin and one that's eight hours old is astounding. If you want the oversized muffin tops you see in the cafés, just grease your muffin pan beforehand to prevent sticking, then add more batter to each muffin case.

225 g/1½ cups plain/all-purpose flour, plus 1 tablespoon for coating the blueberries

200 g/1 cup caster/superfine sugar

1½ teaspoons baking powder

¼ teaspoon salt

50 ml/3 tablespoons milk

40 ml/2 tablespoons double/heavy cream

2 eggs

65 g/4 tablespoons unsalted butter, melted

250 g/2½ cups blueberries, fresh or frozen

Streusel topping

200 g/1½ cups plain/all-purpose flour

70 g/⅓ cup dark brown soft sugar

70 g/⅓ cup caster/superfine sugar

125 g/1 stick chilled unsalted butter, cut into 1-cm/½-inch cubes and chilled

2 teaspoons ground cinnamon

1 teaspoon vanilla extract

a 12-hole muffin pan, lined with muffin cases

Makes 12

Preheat the oven to 180°C (365°F) Gas 6.

Put the flour, sugar, baking powder and salt in a large mixing bowl and stir until well blended. In a separate bowl, combine the milk, cream and eggs. Pour into the flour mixture and stir until just combined. Fold in the melted butter.

In another bowl, toss the blueberries in the extra flour until thoroughly coated, then fold into the muffin batter.

Spoon the mixture into the prepared muffin cases, filling them four-fifths of the way up.

To make the streusel topping, combine all the ingredients and rub with your fingers until nice crumbly, pea-sized balls form. Refrigerate for 10 minutes.

Scatter the streusel topping over the muffins.

Bake in the preheated oven for 25–35 minutes. A wooden skewer inserted in the middle should come out clean, and the tops of the muffins should feel springy to the touch. Remove the muffins from the muffin pan and eat immediately.

LITTLE ALMOND, POLENTA AND LEMON SYRUP CAKES

Polenta is Italian cornmeal and it comes in various grades, ranging from coarse to fine – you want a very fine grade here (which you should be able to find at any Italian deli) for a good dense texture. It's best to eat these cakes on the day you make them, but that shouldn't be too difficult!

140 g/1 cup fine polenta
1 tablespoon baking powder
250 g/1¾ cups ground almonds
225 g/2 sticks unsalted butter, at room temperature
275 g/1 cup golden caster/natural cane sugar
1 tablespoon very finely grated lemon zest
4 eggs

Lemon syrup

115 g/½ cup golden caster/natural cane sugar
2 tablespoons freshly squeezed lemon juice
3 tablespoons flaked/slivered almonds, lightly toasted
icing/confectioners' sugar, to serve

a 12-hole muffin pan, lined with muffin cases

Makes 12

Preheat the oven to 180°C (350°F) Gas 4.

Sift the polenta, baking powder and ground almonds into a large mixing bowl. Tip any pieces of husk into the bowl and make a well in the centre.

In a separate bowl, beat the butter, sugar and lemon zest together until pale and creamy. Add the eggs one at a time, beating well after each addition. Gradually fold in the polenta mixture until well combined.

Spoon the mixture into the prepared muffin pan, dividing it evenly. Bake in the preheated oven for 25 minutes, until risen and golden. Remove from the oven and let cool in the pan for 10 minutes. Carefully transfer the cakes to a wire rack set over a baking sheet (to catch any drips of syrup).

To make the lemon syrup, put the sugar, lemon juice and 2 tablespoons cold water in a small saucepan. Set over low heat and cook, stirring, until the sugar dissolves. Increase the heat to high and bring to the boil, then reduce the heat to a low simmer and cook for 2–3 minutes, until syrupy.

Pour the syrup over the warm cakes. Sprinkle the flaked/slivered almonds on top so they stick to the syrup. Let cool and dust with icing/confectioners' sugar before serving.

COFFEE AND PECAN CUPCAKES WITH PRALINE

These are best made and eaten on the same day, but the undecorated cakes will keep well in the freezer if you want to make a batch to decorate later.

3 tablespoons instant coffee granules

6 tablespoons boiling water

275 g/1¼ cups caster/granulated sugar, plus 2 tablespoons

175 g/1½ sticks unsalted butter, softened and cubed

3 eggs

175 g/1⅓ cups self-raising/rising flour

100 g/⅔ cup pecans, chopped

Frosting

200 g/1 cup icing/confectioners' sugar

2 tablespoons crème fraîche

150 g/1 stick plus 2 tablespoons unsalted butter, softened

2 x 12-hole muffin pans, lined with cupcake cases

a baking sheet, greased and lined with baking parchment

Makes 15

Preheat the oven to 180°C (350°F) Gas 4.

Tip the coffee into a cup with the boiling water and the 2 tablespoons of sugar. Stir together for a minute or so until the sugar has dissolved. Let cool. Put the butter, 175 g/¾ cup of the sugar and the eggs in the bowl of an electric mixer. Sift in the flour, drizzle in 3 tablespoons of the coffee syrup and whisk together for a few minutes to combine. Stir half the pecans into the mixture; reserve the other half for the praline.

Divide the mixture between the cupcake cases. Bake in the preheated oven for 20 minutes, or until risen and lightly golden. Transfer the cupcakes to a wire rack. While they are still warm, make a few fork indentations in the top of each one and carefully drizzle over a little of the remaining coffee syrup, letting it seep into the cakes as you do so. Let cool completely.

Next, make the praline. Tip the remaining 100 g/½ cup sugar into a medium pan or frying pan/skillet over low heat and heat gently. As soon as it has melted, increase the heat a little and let the sugar simmer and gradually turn to a deep golden caramel. Tip in the reserved pecans, give everything a quick stir and tip the hot praline onto the prepared baking sheet. Spread it out slightly, then leave until cold and set.

To make the frosting, sift the icing/confectioners' sugar into a bowl, add the crème fraîche and the butter and beat together until smooth. Spread the frosting onto the cold cupcakes with a round-bladed knife. Bash the praline with the end of a rolling pin to break it up, then crumble some on top of each cake.

DULCE DE LECHE CUPCAKES

Dulce de leche has a butterscotch caramel flavour that goes really well with chocolate. Adding ground almonds and milk chocolate chips to the base of these cupcakes gives them an interesting texture.

Vanilla cupcake mixture

½ vanilla pod/bean

3 eggs

150 g/1 cup icing/confectioners' sugar

150 g/1 cup plus 2 tablespoons plain/all-purpose flour

1 teaspoon baking powder

150 g/1 stick plus 3 tablespoons unsalted butter, melted

45 g/⅓ cup milk/semisweet chocolate chips

30 g/⅓ cup ground almonds

Dulce de leche cream

½ vanilla bean

230 g/⅔ cup dulce de leche, plus extra to drizzle

250 g/9 oz. mascarpone

a cupcake pan, lined with 12 cupcake cases

a piping bag, fitted with a star-shaped nozzle/tip

Makes 12

To make the vanilla cupcake mixture, start the day before you want to back the cupcakes. Split the vanilla bean lengthways and scrape the seeds out into a bowl. Add the eggs and sugar and beat with an electric whisk until tripled in volume and the beaters leave a thick ribbon trail when you lift them out of the mixture.

Sift the flour and baking powder into the bowl and whisk lightly. Add the melted butter and fold in gently with a large metal spoon. Fold in the chocolate chips and ground almonds at the end. Cover and refrigerate for 24 hours.

The next day, preheat the oven to 160°C (325°F) Gas 3.

Divide the mixture between the cupcake cases and bake in the preheated oven for about 15–20 minutes. Remove from the oven and allow to cool completely.

To make the dulce de leche cream, split the vanilla bean lengthways and scrape the seeds out into a bowl. Add the dulce de leche and mix with a balloon whisk or fork to loosen it, then fold in the mascarpone.

Fill the piping bag with the cream and pipe on top of the cold cupcakes. Drizzle dulce de leche on top.

MADE-IN-FRANCE WHOOPIES

In the Brittany region of France, 'caramel au beurre salé' – salted caramel – is a local speciality. These chocolate whoopies with salted caramel cream honour this delicious delicacy.

Chocolate whoopie shells

6 eggs, separated

170 g/generous ¾ cup caster/superfine sugar

130 g/1 cup plain/all-purpose flour

40 g/scant ½ cup cocoa powder

Salted caramel cream

100 ml/⅓ cup plus 1 tablespoon single/light cream

100 g/3½ oz. chewy toffee sweets/candy, plus extra, chopped, to fill

25 g/2 tablespoons salted butter

200 g/7 oz. mascarpone

a piping bag, fitted with a plain nozzle/tip

a baking sheet, greased and lined with baking parchment

Makes about 15

Preheat the oven to 190°C (375°F) Gas 5.

To make the chocolate whoopie shells, put the egg whites and sugar in a grease-free stainless-steel mixing bowl and whisk with an electric whisk until white and glossy and stiff peaks have formed. Lightly beat the egg yolks in a separate bowl to loosen them, then gently fold into the egg whites with a large metal spoon. Sift in the flour and cocoa powder and fold in until evenly incorporated.

Fill the piping bag with the mixture. Pipe about 30 large rounds of the mixture on the prepared baking sheet. Space the rounds roughly 6 cm/2½ inches apart. Alternatively, you can spoon the mixture neatly onto the baking sheet using 2 tablespoons.

Bake in the preheated oven for about 12 minutes. Remove from the oven and allow to cool on the baking sheet.

To make the salted caramel cream, pour the cream into a saucepan and gently bring to the boil. Add the toffee sweets/candy and cook over low–medium heat until all the toffees have melted. Now add the butter and stir until melted and smooth. Transfer to a bowl, allow to cool slightly, then refrigerate.

Add the mascarpone to the chilled salted caramel and whisk with the electric whisk just until the caramel is evenly incorporated. Fill the piping bag with the salted caramel cream. Pipe a small amount onto the flat underside of half of the cold whoopie pies. Add some chopped toffees and sandwich with another whoopie pie shell.

MADELEINES

These lovely little cakes, shaped like scallop shells, are believed to have originated in the Lorraine region of France. Since Marcel Proust gave them a mention in his novel 'Remembrance of Things Past', generations of French children have come home from school to a plate of these to dip in their 'chocolat chaud'. They work equally well with a nice cup of coffee.

130 g/1 cup plain/all-purpose flour
½ teaspoon baking powder
a pinch of salt
120 g/⅔ cup caster/granulated sugar
3 eggs
2 teaspoons honey
grated zest of 1 lemon
120 g/1 stick salted butter, melted and cooled
1 tablespoon icing/ confectioners' sugar, to decorate

a non-stick madeleine pan, buttered and floured

Makes about 24

Preheat the oven to 190°C (375°F) Gas 5.

Sift the flour, baking powder and salt into a bowl and set aside.

In a large bowl, whisk the sugar, eggs, honey and lemon zest with an electric hand whisk until it has tripled in volume and the mixture leaves a thick ribbon trail when you lift the beaters. Add the sifted dry ingredients and whisk lightly. Add the melted butter and fold in until just incorporated.

Spoon the mixture into the prepared pan. You should have about half the mixture remaining – cover with clingfilm/plastic wrap and refrigerate until later. Bake the madeleines in the preheated oven for 15 minutes. Remove from the oven and turn out onto a wire rack to cool.

Wash, butter and flour the madeleine pan, fill with the remaining mixture and bake as before. Eat the first batch whilst waiting for the second to bake! Dust with icing/confectioners' sugar to serve.

The madeleines are best eaten on the day of baking, or can be frozen for up to 2 months.

SAFFRON RING CAKE

Ring cakes are popular all over Italy; the beauty of them is their simplicity. This pretty saffron-speckled version is a favourite, inspired by the fabulous saffron grown in L'Aquila in the region of Abruzzo. Using cream to provide the fat element in the cake gives it a lovely flavour, which combines superbly with the saffron, creating a delicate and delicious cake that is perfect with a steaming hot cup of morning coffee.

250 ml/1 cup whipping cream
a large pinch of saffron
3 eggs, beaten
250 g/2 cups self-raising/rising
    flour
250 g/1¼ cups caster/
    granulated sugar
a pinch of salt

*a ring-shaped cake pan,
    buttered*

Serves 8

Preheat the oven to 180°C (350°F) Gas 4.

Pour the cream into a saucepan and add the saffron. Bring the mixture to simmering point, then turn off the heat and leave the saffron to infuse for 10 minutes.

Let the cream mixture cool and pour it into a large bowl. Whisk in the eggs, then add the flour, sugar and salt and stir well until everything is thoroughly combined.

Spoon the mixture into the prepared pan and bake for about 40 minutes, until the cake is risen and golden and springs back when prodded gently with an index finger.

CRUMBLY LEMON CAKE

A gorgeous, lemony, crumbly-but-crunchy cake, which is a speciality of Ferrara in the north of Italy. Traditionally it is never cut, but simply broken into pieces to share. For fans of all things lemony, this cake should really carry a health warning because it is seriously addictive.

120 g/1 stick unsalted butter, cubed

170 g/1⅓ cups plain/all-purpose flour

120 g/½ cup plus 2 tablespoons caster/superfine sugar

120 g/¾ cup ground almonds

100 g/⅔ cup fine polenta/cornmeal or semolina

grated zest of 2 unwaxed lemons

2 egg yolks, beaten

a 23-cm/9-inch loose-bottomed cake pan, buttered

Serves 6–8

Preheat the oven to 180°C (350°F) Gas 4.

Rub the butter, flour and sugar together until the mixture resembles fine breadcrumbs. Stir in the ground almonds and polenta. Add the lemon zest and mix well.

Work in the egg yolks; at this point the mixture will become a little lumpy. Scatter the mixture evenly into the prepared pan, but do not press it down. Bake for about 45 minutes, until golden and firm. Remove from the oven and leave to cool, breaking into pieces to serve. To keep the lemon cake crunchy, it's best stored in an airtight tin.

BLACKCURRANT, BERRY AND HAZELNUT CRUMBLE CAKE

This recipe also works well using damson jam/jelly. Either way, treat yourself to some chilled Greek yogurt on the side.

150 g/1 stick plus 2 tablespoons butter, softened

175 g/¾ cup caster/granulated sugar

2 eggs

125 g/1 cup self-raising/rising flour

50 g/⅓ cup polenta/cornmeal

1 teaspoon baking powder

finely grated zest of 1 small unwaxed lemon

50 g/¼ cup Greek yogurt

175 g/¾ cup blackcurrant jam/jelly

175 g/1¼ cups raspberries

Crumble topping

100 g/⅔ cup shelled, blanched hazelnuts

75 g/⅓ cup demerara sugar

75 g/5 tablespoons unsalted butter, chilled and cubed

100 g/¾ cup self-raising/rising flour

a 23-cm/9-inch springform pan, 6 cm/2½ inch deep, greased and lined with baking parchment

Serves 12

Preheat the oven to 180°C (350°F) Gas 4.

To make the crumble topping, chop the nuts by hand or pulse them in a food processor – you want them to be roughly chopped. Mix the sugar, butter and flour in an electric mixer until combined, then add 1–2 tablespoons cold water and briefly whiz again until the mixture resembles breadcrumbs. Mix in the nuts. Alternatively, you can rub the butter into the flour by hand in a mixing bowl, then stir in the sugar, water and nuts. Set aside.

Put the butter, sugar, eggs, flour, polenta/cornmeal, baking powder, lemon zest and Greek yogurt in an electric mixer and mix until combined.

Spoon the mixture into the prepared pan and spread it evenly. Tip the jam/jelly into a bowl and mix it with a spoon to loosen it, then put spoonfuls over the top of the cake mixture. Using the tip of a round-bladed knife, gently spread the jam/jelly by lightly swirling it into the top of the cake mixture. Sprinkle a third of the crumble mixture on top, scatter the raspberries over this, then finish with the remaining crumble topping.

Put the pan on a baking sheet and bake in the preheated oven for 1 hour 5 minutes–1 hour 10 minutes, until just set in the middle. Let cool in the pan before releasing it, removing the baking parchment and transferring to a plate or board to slice.

RICH CHOCOLATE AND ALMOND CAKE

This recipe is based on an irresistibly rich chocolate cake that originally came from Capri, the island just off the tip of the Sorrento Peninsula. If they have caffès in heaven, this is sure to be on the menu. Serve in thin slices with a good espresso.

200 g/1 cup caster/granulated sugar

4 eggs, separated

200 g/1 stick plus 6 tablespoons unsalted butter, melted and cooled

200 g/6½ oz. dark/bittersweet chocolate, finely chopped

250 g/1⅔ cup almonds, finely chopped

2 tablespoons Strega liqueur (optional)

icing/confectioners' sugar, for dusting

a 23-cm/9-inch loose-bottomed cake pan, greased and lined with baking parchment

Serves 8–10

Preheat the oven to 180°C (350°F) Gas 4.

Beat the sugar and egg yolks together until light and fluffy.

Stir in the cooled melted butter and then the chocolate and almonds. Add the Strega at this point, if using.

In a clean bowl, whisk the egg whites until firm. Fold them lightly but thoroughly into the almond mixture until they are fully incorporated. Spoon the mixture into the prepared pan and cook for about 30 minutes (the cake will be slightly squidgy in the centre). Remove from the oven and leave to cool in the pan.

Dust with icing/confectioners' sugar and serve.

CHOCOLATE AND HAZELNUT TORTE

This dark and creamy cake makes an ideal dessert. Ground hazelnuts bring a sophisticated flavour that combines perfectly with dark chocolate.

100 g/⅔ cup whole, blanched
  hazelnuts
250 g/8½ oz. dark/bittersweet
  chocolate, roughly chopped
100 g/7 tablespoons salted
  butter
6 eggs, separated
½ teaspoon cream of tartar
120 g/⅔ cup caster/granulated
  sugar

Topping
200 g/6½ oz. dark/bittersweet
  chocolate, roughly chopped
125 g/1 stick salted butter
4 tablespoons whole, blanched
  hazelnuts

*a 23-cm/9-inch round, loose-
  based cake pan, greased and
  lined with baking parchment*

Serves 10–12

Preheat the oven to 170°C (325°F) Gas 3.

Toast the hazelnuts for both the cake and the topping in the preheated oven for 10 minutes. Keep any eye on them to make sure they are not burning. Allow to cool, then set aside the 4 tablespoons for the topping and grind the remaining nuts to a fine powder in a food processor. Melt the chocolate and butter in a heatproof bowl set over a pan of barely simmering water. Do not let the base of the bowl touch the water. Let cool.

In a bowl, beat the egg yolks together with a balloon or electric hand whisk for 2 minutes, or until they become pale in colour. In a separate large bowl, and with a clean whisk, beat the egg whites and cream of tartar together until soft peaks are formed. Add the sugar in stages, beating continually, until stiff peaks are formed.

Add the beaten egg yolks to the melted butter and chocolate and whisk lightly. Add half the egg whites to this mixture and gently fold together with a spatula. Transfer this mixture to the bowl with the remaining egg whites, add the ground hazelnuts and gently fold everything together.

Spoon the mixture into the prepared cake pan and bake in the preheated oven for 50 minutes or until a skewer inserted into the middle of the torte comes out clean. Allow to cool completely before removing from the pan.

To make the topping, melt the chocolate and butter together as described above. Add 2 tablespoons warm water and stir until smooth. Remove the bowl from the pan and allow to cool. Spread over the top of the torte using a palette knife. Roughly chop the reserved roasted hazelnuts and sprinkle them over the middle of the torte, to decorate.

COFFEE, PECAN AND MAPLE CAKE

A twist on the classic coffee and walnut cake, this light, golden sponge is rich with the flavour of toasted pecans and filled with a sweet, buttery frosting with a hint of coffee and maple syrup.

180 g/1½ sticks unsalted butter, at room temperature

180 g/¾ cup caster/granulated sugar

3 eggs

180 g/1¼ cups self-raising/rising flour

2 teaspoons instant coffee granules dissolved in 1 tablespoon just-boiled water

60 g/½ cup pecans, roughly chopped

Frosting

100 g/7 tablespoons butter, at room temperature

2 tablespoons maple syrup

2 teaspoons instant coffee granules dissolved in 1 tablespoon just-boiled water

200 g/1⅓ cups icing/confectioners' sugar, sifted

whole pecans, to decorate

2 x 20-cm/8-inch springform cake pans, greased and lined with baking parchment

Serves 8

Preheat the oven to 180°C (350°F) Gas 4.

Beat together the butter and sugar until pale and creamy, then beat in the eggs, one at a time. Sift over the flour and fold in, then fold in the coffee and pecans.

Divide the mixture between the prepared cake pans and spread out in an even layer. Bake for about 20 minutes until golden and a skewer inserted in the centre comes out clean.

Turn out on to a wire rack and leave to cool completely.

To make the frosting, beat the butter until creamy, then add the maple syrup and coffee and sift over half the icing/confectioners' sugar. Beat together until smooth and creamy, then gradually beat in the remaining icing/confectioners' sugar.

Put one of the cakes on a serving plate and slice a thin layer off the top to create a flat surface. Spread slightly less than half the frosting over the top. Put the second cake on the filling and spread the remaining frosting over the top. Decorate with the pecans.

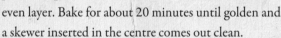

MOCHA SWIRL CAKE WITH ESPRESSO ICING

The fromage frais in this loaf keeps the fat content down and the polenta gives it a lovely crunchy crust.

1 slightly rounded tablespoon espresso instant coffee powder

1 tablespoon boiling water

200 g/¾ cup fromage frais

75 g/½ cup polenta/cornmeal

125 g/1 stick unsalted butter, softened

225 g/1 cup caster/granulated sugar

3 eggs

200 g/1⅔ cups self-raising/rising flour

½ teaspoon bicarbonate of/ baking soda

1 teaspoon vanilla extract

2 teaspoons cocoa powder

Espresso icing

100 g/⅔ cup icing/ confectioners' sugar

1 slightly rounded teaspoon espresso instant coffee powder

a 19 x 9 x 7-cm/7½ x 3½ x 3-inch loaf pan, greased and lined with baking parchment

Serves 8–10

Preheat the oven to 180°C (350°F) Gas 4.

Put the espresso powder and boiling water in a cup and stir to dissolve, then let cool.

Next, take a scant tablespoon from the fromage frais and set it aside for the icing. Put the remaining fromage frais with the polenta/cornmeal, butter, sugar, eggs, flour and bicarbonate of/baking soda in an electric mixer (or use a large mixing bowl and an electric whisk) and beat until combined. Transfer half the mixture to another bowl. Stir the vanilla extract into the first bowl. Stir the dissolved coffee and the cocoa into the second bowl.

Spoon the 2 mixtures into the prepared loaf pan in 3 layers, alternating spoonfuls of each mixture in each layer to resemble a chequerboard. Finally, using a skewer, gently swirl the layers together a few times until you have a definite swirl pattern on top of the loaf.

Bake in the preheated oven for 55 minutes, or until risen and the loaf is a lovely golden colour on top. Let cool in the pan.

To make the espresso icing, sift the icing/confectioners' sugar into a bowl and mix in the espresso powder along with the reserved tablespoon of fromage frais. Add enough cold water to make the icing a spreadable consistency – about 2 teaspoonfuls – but add it gradually, stirring, as you might not need it all.

Run a knife around the edges of the cold loaf in the pan to release it. Turn it out, remove the baking parchment and spread the icing on top of the loaf. Let set before slicing.

ALMOND AND PISTACHIO CAKE

A damp, delicious and very dangerous cake, this, because it's hard to stop at just one slice. Try cutting the slices in half – then you won't feel so bad if you have two!

250 g/2 sticks plus 1 tablespoon
    unsalted butter, softened
200 g/1 cup caster/granulated
    sugar
4 eggs, beaten
120 g/¾ cup ground almonds
100 g/⅔ cup ground pistachios
50 g/5 tablespoons plain/
    all-purpose flour
1 teaspoon baking powder
grated zest of 2 unwaxed
    lemons

Pistachio topping

60 g/5 tablespoons
    caster/granulated sugar
freshly squeezed juice of
    2 lemons
60 g/½ cup pistachios, chopped

*a 900-g/9 x 5 x 3-inch loaf pan,
    greased and lined with baking
    parchment*

Serves 10–12

Preheat the oven to 180°C (350°F) Gas 4.

Beat the butter and sugar together until smooth. Add the eggs, a little at a time, and beat until fully incorporated.

Stir in the ground almonds and pistachios, the flour, the baking powder and the lemon zest. Spoon the mixture into the prepared pan and bake for about 45 minutes, until a skewer inserted into the centre of the cake comes out clean. Remove from the oven.

Meanwhile, make the topping. Heat the caster/granulated sugar and lemon juice in a saucepan. Stir in the pistachios. When the sugar has completely dissolved, pour the mixture evenly over the cake. Leave to cool in the pan and then turn out and serve cut into slices.

GINGER CAKE

This recipe is deliciously aromatic, with a lovely texture. If you can't find ground cloves, you can use whole ones and then grind them as finely as possible with a pestle and mortar or in a spice mill.

300 g/2 sticks plus 5 tablespoons unsalted butter, softened at room temperature
250 g/1¼ cups light muscovado sugar
3 teaspoons vanilla extract
5 eggs
3 teaspoons baking powder
1½ teaspoons ground cinnamon
1½ teaspoons ground cloves
3 teaspoons cardamom seeds, crushed with a pestle and mortar
1½ teaspoons ground ginger
300 g/2⅓ cups plain/all-purpose flour

an 18-cm/7-inch loose-bottomed/springform cake pan, greased

Serves 12–16

Preheat the oven to 180°C (350°F) Gas 4.

Put the butter and sugar in a large mixing bowl and cream with a wooden spoon or handheld electric whisk until pale and fluffy. Stir in the vanilla extract. Add the eggs one by one, whisking well after each addition.

In a separate bowl, sift the baking powder, spices and flour together, then fold into the egg mixture.

Spoon the mixture into the prepared cake pan and level the top with the back of the spoon.

Bake in the preheated oven for 50–60 minutes, until the cake is firm to the touch and a skewer inserted into the centre comes out clean. The cake tastes best the day after baking and is also suitable for freezing.

INDEX

RECIPE CREDITS

Mickael Benichou
bonjour brownies
coffee lover's brownies
dulce de leche cupcakes
made-in-France whoopies
orange crush cookies

Susannah Blake
cappuccino cheesecake
coffee and cinnamon rolls
coffee bean and cherry biscotti
coffee, macadamia and white chocolate
    chunk cookies
coffee, pecan and maple cake

Julian Day
amaretti biscuits
bakewell slices
chocolate and hazelnut torte
chocolate fudge brownies
chocolate tiffin
chocolate, ginger and orange slices
fig and marsala crostata
madeleines
pecan and chocolate tart

Ross Dobson
almond, polenta and lemon syrup cakes

Liz Franklin
almond and pistachio cake
caramel almond cookies
cherry and almond tart
chocolate and almond tartlets
chocolate and pear tart
coffee and chocolate tart
crumbly lemon cake
individual apple tarts
ladies' kisses
rich chocolate and almond cake

ricotta doughnuts
saffron ring cake
toasted hazelnut florentines

Jane Mason
autumnal sticky buns
chocolate sticks
Mexican coffee buns
monkey buns
vigilantes

Hannah Miles
Austrian apricot doughnuts
bombolini
caramel ring doughnuts
caramel shortbread
coffee cream doughnuts
coffee religieuse
cruellers
flapjack pecan brownies
Paris Brest
pistachio triangle doughnuts
plum and almond puffs
strudel cream puffs

Miisa Mink
almond twists
Boston cake
ginger cake

Isidora Popovic
chocolate and pear tart
ginger and chilli caramel cookies
hazelnut macaroons
pecan and bourbon tartlets
pecan and cranberry cookies
white chocolate and coffee truffle
    brownies
white chocolate and fig biscuits

Sarah Randell
blackcurrant, berry and hazelnut crumble
    cake
chocolate fudge raspberry shortbread
chocolate heaven muffins
coffee and pear cupcakes with praline
hazelnut, orange and Marsala raisin
    biscotti
honey, toasted pine nut and pumpkin seed
    flapjacks with chocolate topping
mocha swirl cake
no-bake chocolate, macadamia and fig
    slices
pear, mascarpone and orange tartlets
pecan cheesecake swirl brownies
prune, cinnamon and toasted walnut
    cookies
toffee bars

Annie Rigg
coffee blondies
salted caramel swirl brownies

Bea Vo
almond cherry muffins
blueberry streusel muffins
chocolate peanut butter biscotti
chocolate peanut butter cheesecake
German chocolate cheesecake
rocky road fudge bars
ultimate chocolate chip cookies

Laura Washburn
apple spice muffins
apple, fig and nut bars
praline apple strudel

PICTURE CREDITS